C000281440

The past revealed
GREAT DISCOVERIES IN ARCHAEOLOGY

WHITE STAR PUBLISHERS

text

MARK ROSE
ETI BONN-MULLER
GIORGIO FERRERO

project editor
VALERIA MANFERTO DE FABIANIS

editorial coordination
GIORGIO FERRERO

graphic design
MARINELLA DEBERNARDI

1 Following his exploratory travels through Cambodia in the late 19th century, French artist Louis Delaporte
drew this sketch of the Angkor ruins.

4 This photograph from the late 19th century depicts the Lion Gate of Mycenae during the first excavation season.

6 One of the greatest masterpieces of classical Greek statuary, this bronze statue, known simply as "A," was found
off the coast of Riace (Calabria) in 1972 (National Museum, Reggio Calabria).

Contents

Introduction

Archaeology is the thrilling story of great discoveries such as the gold funerary mask of the 18th Dynasty Pharaoh Tutankhamun and the jade one of Pakal, the 7th-century A.D. ruler of Palenque. And spectacular finds that archaeologists have made in the past, like the Assyrian palace at Nineveh, can be matched today by the mapping and recovery of the submerged ruins of the Ptolemaic capital of Alexandria.

But archaeological discovery is not the province of scholars alone. Adventurers and explorers have played their role as well. A hundred years or more ago, Johann Burckhardt was the first European to set eyes on the ruins of Petra, and Hiram Bingham brought Machu Picchu into the international limelight. Tales of chance finds—a stray goat leading to the Dead Sea Scrolls, an unemployed metal detector enthusiast stumbling on a huge Anglo-Saxon hoard—continue to amaze and inspire.

And there will always be room for dissenters in the academic community. By 1920, archaeologists thought that the Valley of the Kings, Egypt's royal burial ground, was exhausted. However, Howard Carter was convinced that the tomb of at least one pharaoh, Tutankhamun, had not yet been found. On a fateful day in November 1922, his workers brought to light limestone steps that led to a doorway, still plastered with mud and stamped with the mark of the priests of the necropolis: a seal depicting a jackal and nine captives. "At first I could see nothing, the hot air escaping from the chamber causing the candle flame to flicker," Carter later recalled, "but presently, as my eyes grew accustomed to the light, details of the room within emerged slowly from the mist, strange animals, statues, and gold—everywhere the glint of gold."

But archaeology is not always about finding the glamorous treasures of kings. Among the most haunting discoveries ever made are the fossilized residents of Pompeii and Herculaneum, frozen in the moment that they attempted to flee the blistering ash that rained down following the A.D. 79 eruption of Mount Vesuvius. Pliny the Younger, a teenage eyewitness to the horrifying scene, later recorded the events in chilling detail: "You could hear the howls of women, the wailing of babies, and the shouts of men...there were some who in their fear of dying begged for death."

These sites were abandoned in antiquity and nearly forgotten until March 1748, when surveying engineer Rocco Gioacchino de Alcubiere began to investigate Pompeii (and later Herculaneum) on a treasure-hunting mission for the Spanish royal court. His excavations eventually caught the attention of Johann Winckelmann, a German scholar and lover of ancient Greece, who is widely regarded as the first art historian. Winckelmann, who famously detailed his visits to the sites, also came to be known as the father of modern classical archaeology. He later wrote of his frustrations over how these early excavations were being conducted: "The subterranean works at Pompeii are those that promise most, for here they are not only sure of proceeding step by step in a great city, but have found out the principal street of it...[The work, however, is being] carried on in a very slow and indolent manner...Great a city as Pompeii is known to have been, I, in my last journey, found but eight men at work on the ruins of it."

Archaeology also seeks to unravel ancient mysteries and to chart the course of human history. "Great question has arisen from whence came those aboriginal inhabitants of America," wrote Thomas Jefferson in *Notes on the State of Virginia* (1781). "[The] late discoveries of Captain Cook, coasting from Kamchatka to California, have proved that, if the two continents of Asia and America be separated at all, it is only by a narrow strait. So that from this side also, inhabitants may have passed into America: and the resemblance between the Indians of America and the Eastern inhabitants of Asia, would induce us to conjecture, that the former are the descendants of the later, or the later of the former." Jefferson went looking for the explanation of how the New World was colonized, and his subsequent 1784 excavation of a

burial mound in western Virginia is considered the first scientific archaeological dig. But the concept of archaeology is much older than Jefferson.

The philosopher Plato (428–348 B.C.) used the word *archaiologia* in his dialogue *Hippias Major*, in which Socrates is engaged in a discussion about a definition of beauty with the well-traveled sophist Hippias, who notes that the Spartans are interested in only one subject:

Socrates: "Well, just what is it they love to hear about from you and applaud? Tell me yourself; I can't figure it out."

Hippias: "The genealogies of heroes and men, Socrates, and the settlements [how cities were founded in ancient times], and in a word all 'archaiologia'—that's what they most love to hear about."

The Spartans weren't alone among the Greeks in their interest in the ancient world. The 5th-century B.C. historian Herodotus, one of the first tourists, recorded various theories about how the Great Pyramids of Giza were built two millennia before. The 1st-century A.D. historian Pausanias visited the imposing Late Bronze Age sites of Mycenae and Tiryns, noting, "Still, there are parts of the city wall left, including the gate with lions standing on it. They say this is the work of the Kyklopes, who built the wall of Tiryns."

The Romans, however, were among the first to collect the ancient monuments and artifacts of Greece, Asia Minor, and Egypt. They plundered the graves of ancient Corinth for artifacts that they used to decorate their homes. And inscriptions on a 6th-century B.C. Egyptian obelisk—brought to Rome in the 1st or 2nd century A.D. and still standing in the Piazza della Minerva—would play a key role in deciphering hieroglyphs.

Some 18 centuries later, the love for antiquities was rekindled when Napoleon Bonaparte and the scholars who accompanied his expedition in 1798 rediscovered ancient Egypt. Soon afterward, all Europe was enthralled by accounts such as Dominique Vivant Denon's *Travels in Upper and Lower Egypt*. There was suddenly a demand by European museums and collectors for Egypt-ian antiquities. Among the early explorers to gather and ship back artifacts was Giovanni Belzoni who was as much adventurer as archaeologist:

"After getting through these passages, some of them two or three hundred yards long, you generally find a more commodious place, perhaps high enough to sit. But what a place of rest! Surrounded by bodies, by heaps of mummies in all directions; which, previous to my being accustomed to the sight, impressed me with horror…In such a situation I found myself several times, and often returned exhausted and fainting, till at last I became inured to it, and indifferent to what I suffered, except from the dust, which never failed to choke my throat and nose; and though, fortunately, I am destitute of the sense of smelling, I could taste that the mummies were rather unpleasant to swallow."

Others went looking for legendary sites based on ancient texts. In the 1870s, Heinrich Schliemann—obsessed, eccentric, and wealthy—was determined to prove that the Trojan War was not merely a myth. When he unearthed a gold mask at Mycenae, he was said to have claimed that he had "gazed upon the face of Agamemnon." During his earlier excavation at Troy, he unearthed a fantastic Early Bronze Age treasure, which he believed was that of the doomed Trojan king Priam. In his account of the discovery, he wrote:

"While the men were eating and resting, I cut out the treasure with a large knife, which it was impossible to do without the very greatest exertion and the most fearful risk of my life, for the great fortification-wall, beneath which I had to dig, threatened every moment to fall down upon me. But the sight of so many objects, every one of which is of inestimable value to archaeology, made me foolhardy, and I never thought of any danger. It would, however, have been impossible for me to have removed the treasure without the help of my dear wife, who stood by me ready to pack the things which I cut out in her shawl and to carry them away."

His wife, Sophia, later modeled the jewelry from the treasure, as she posed for photographs.

Schliemann inspired others to learn more about the pre-classical Greece that had first come to light under his spade. At the turn of the century, Sir Arthur Evans excavated the palace at Knossos, becoming the first to discover the great civilization of Bronze Age Crete, which he named "Minoan," after its legendary King Minos. "Consider for a moment the services rendered within quite recent years by what has been called Prehistoric Archaeology, but which in truth was never more Historic, in widening the horizon of our past," he said of the discovery in a speech. "It has drawn aside the curtain, and revealed the dawn. It has dispelled, like the unsubstantial phantoms of a dream, those preconceived notions as to the origin of human arts and institutions at which Epicurus and Lucretius already laughed, before the days of Biblical chronology."

The ruins of great New World civilizations were also being explored during the 19th century. John Stephens, an astute observer and writer, and Frederick Catherwood, a talented artist, pioneered the accurate description and recording of the Maya cities of Central America and Mexico. In his account of the 9th-century A.D. city of Labná, Stephens wrote in his *Incidents of Travel in Yucatán* (1848):

"The figures and ornaments on this wall were painted; the remains of bright colours are still visible, defying the action of the elements. If a solitary traveller from the Old World could by some strange accident have visited this aboriginal city when it was yet perfect, his account would have seemed more fanciful than any in Eastern story, and been considered a subject for the Arabian Nights' Entertainments."

If the 19th century was one of rediscovery, the early 20th century was a golden age of large-scale excavations, such as those at Ur, the Biblical birthplace of Abraham, directed by Leonard Woolley. Although he employed as many as 300 local workers, Woolley was a meticulous excavator. In his very first season, in 1922, he discovered Ur's royal cemetery, which would prove to hold thousands of burials and treasures to equal Tutankhamun's. But Wool-

ley understood the importance of unearthing the finds properly, and shifted his untried crew to digging ancient mud-brick buildings instead. The careful work of excavating the burials, he said, "Could not be done satisfactorily with the absolutely untrained gang which we had just enrolled." It was only four years later that he returned to the cemetery—with workers who were then able to meet the challenge.

Some of the greatest archaeological discoveries have been made by chance, including the terracotta army of Qin Shihuangdi, the first emperor of China. Found in 1974 by farmers digging wells in search of water, the clay warriors and horses—believed to be some 8,000 strong—along with their bronze chariots and weapons, came to light after secretly guarding the tomb of the great ruler for more than two millennia. While the discovery of thousands of these unique figures near Xi'an captured the world's attention, the emperor's wondrous final resting place, as described by 2nd-century B.C. Chinese historian Sima Qian, still lies underground. In his *Shiji* (*Historical Records*), he wrote of the burial:

"In the ninth month the First Emperor was interred at Mt. Li. When the emperor first came to the throne he began digging and shaping Mt. Li. Later, when he unified the empire, he had over 700,000 men from all over the empire transported to the spot. They dug down to the third layer of underground springs and poured in bronze to make the outer coffin. Replicas of palaces, scenic towers, and the hundred officials, as well as rare utensils and wonderful objects, were brought to fill up the tomb. Craftsmen were ordered to set up crossbows and arrows, rigged so they would immediately shoot down anyone attempting to break in. Mercury was used to fashion imitations of the hundred rivers, the Yellow River and the Yangtze, and the seas, constructed in such a way that they seemed to flow. Above were representations of all the heavenly bodies, below, the features of the earth. Fish oil was used for lamps, which were calculated to burn for a long time without going out."

Following Woolley, Chinese archaeologists are in no rush to dig the first emperor's tomb. It will wait, and excavation methods and technology will only improve in the meanwhile.

The invention of scuba gear, and more recently of deep-sea robotic vehicles, means that some of the greatest discoveries are today being made underwater. Around the same time as the Xi'an warriors emerged from their earthy tomb, an amateur diver—a chemist on holiday from Rome—made an extraordinarily lucky find off the coast of Riace, near Reggio Calabria. The stiff hand on the seafloor he originally thought belonged to a corpse, turned out to be affixed to one of a pair of rare and exquisite classical bronze warriors, expertly fashioned by a Greek sculptor and likely lost as they were being transported by ship during a violent storm.

The accessibility of sites can endanger them when looters strike. In 1987, more than a decade after the Riace find, Walter Alva uncovered a Moche ceremonial center near the village of Sipán in Peru that had been lost for 1,000 years. The artifacts from its splendid royal tombs—including gold masks, necklaces of gold and silver, and ear spools of gold and turquoise—were brought to the attention of researchers when Peruvian police seized a cache during the raid of a well-known *huaquero* (grave robber). "A site like this is an archaeologist's dream," said Alva. Not only in times of peace, but also—and especially—during conflicts ancient sites need to be protected.

The plunder of the Kuwait National Museum in 1990 and the damage done to Iraq's museums and ancient sites in recent years are sad examples of this, but Afghanistan must also be remembered. Its national museum, 6 miles (10 km) south of Kabul, was often on the front line during the wars leading to the collapse of the Soviet-backed government and the rise of the Taliban in 1996. Most of the collection—including a Greco-Bactrian hoard of more than 600 coins from Kunduz, carved ivories from Begram, and more than 20,000 gold ornaments dated from 1st century B.C. to the 1st century A.D. excavated at Tillya Tepe—

was believed lost. Fears increased in 2001, when the Taliban destroyed the colossal Buddhas at Bamiyan. But in 2003, the Tillya Tepe gold and the museum's other masterpieces reappeared. In 1988, the precious relics had been stored in the vault of the central bank. Since then, Omar Khan Massoudi, director of Kabul's national museum, and a few others had risked their lives to protect the artifacts, keeping the gold hidden away from all of the warring factions for some 15 years.

Today we face a dilemma. Will we protect our heritage or not? Great vistas are being opened by new technologies. Geophysical prospecting can expose what is below the surface of the ground even before digging begins, while satellite imagery can reveal ancient caravan routes and the walls of cities that are thousands of years old. Bone chemistry studies can pinpoint where an individual grew up, and DNA analysis can tell us what their lineage was and what diseases they suffered from. Discoveries not thought possible a decade ago are now within reach. But amassing raw data, however sophisticated the means, is not the goal of archaeology.

"If there be a connecting theme in the following pages, it is this: an insistence that the archaeologist is digging up, not things, but people. Unless the bits and pieces with which he deals be alive to him, unless he have himself the common touch, he had better seek out other disciplines for his exercise," wrote Mortimer Wheeler in his classic *Archaeology from the Earth* a half-century ago. "In a simple direct sense, archaeology is a science that must be lived, must be 'seasoned with humanity.' Dead archaeology is the driest dust that blows."

We agree. On the following pages, you'll find some of the most important, exciting, and defining discoveries in archaeology, richly illustrated with iconic photographs and historic drawings. As you read about these great finds and the people who made them, we hope you'll uncover your favorites and let your imagination wander as you realize how much is yet to be discovered. (MR and EBM)

The Great Archaeologists

Henry Layard

Heinrich Schliemann

Robert Koldewey

Arthur Evans

Leonard Woolley

Max Uhle

Ernesto Schiaparelli

Ludwig Borchardt

Howard Carter

Pierre Montet

Alberto Ruz Lhuillier

Manolis Andronikos

Viktor Sarianidi

Walter Alva

Paolo Matthiae

Jean-Yves Empereur

Zahi Hawass

What makes an archaeologist great? Is it his or her unquenchable desire to explore uncharted ruins, uncanny knowledge of just where to dig, insistence on excavating scientifically, or ability to publish a field report in a timely manner? There are many definitions of archaeological greatness, and all of the individuals outlined in this chapter have done something truly great. They've uncovered lost civilizations, brought to light spectacular treasures, or conducted digs at sites so groundbreaking that they've literally rewritten—and in some cases written—the history books. The reasons for their greatness are as varied as the countries from which they hail.

There have been a number of brilliant British excavators. Austen Henry Layard, a successful politician and diplomat, is best known as the excavator of the Assyrian sites of Nimrud and Nineveh in the 1840s. His legacy is based on the great reliefs and sculptures he recovered for the British Museum and for his numerous books known for their lively writing, such as *Nineveh and Its Remains*, which was a bestseller and introduced Assyrian culture to the world. In 1900, Arthur Evans began excavating the palace of Knossos on Crete, thus illuminating the extraordinary Bronze Age civilization of the Minoans. Knighted in 1911 for his contributions to the field of archaeology, Evans will always be remembered for imaginatively melding myth and reality in his interpretations and for helping to ignite a passion for the study of a pre-classical Greece.

Then there is Howard Carter who will forever be linked to the young Pharaoh Tutankhamun. Carter's 1922 discovery of the Boy King's unplundered tomb yielded extraordinary treasures, which required careful documentation and handling. Where Carter took years to do this, most of his contemporaries would have taken mere weeks. Leonard Woolley, educated at Oxford, led the joint British Museum and University of Pennsylvania Museum expedition at Ur. In 1927, he uncovered the burials of the kings and queens of Ur, the home of the Biblical patriarch Abraham. Dating to 2600–2500 B.C., the Royal Cemetery tombs mark a high point in Sumerian culture.

The Germans also had a great impact on the early development of the field of archaeology. For better or worse, a list of great German archaeologists must surely include Heinrich Schliemann, who is one of archaeology's most controversial figures. He invented history when it suited it him; for example, claiming that his wife Sophia helped him excavate Priam's Treasure at Troy in 1873 but later admitting she was not present. And he took credit for the ideas of others, notably Frank Calvert who owned a part of the site of ancient Troy. At the same time, Schliemann was a pioneer, employing specialists to identify animal remains at Troy and analyze the sources of amber found at Mycenae. But there were others whose reputations remain intact.

In 1896, Max Uhle began investigating the site of Pachacamac, just south of Lima, Peru, where his discovery of "mummy bales" captivated the world's attention. He will always be remembered as the father of Andean archaeology. Around the same time, but half a world away, Robert Koldewey was unearthing the ancient city of Babylon in Iraq, where he claimed to have found the legendary Tower of Babel. Some years later, Ludwig Borchardt excavated at Amarna, the capital of the "heretic" Pharaoh Akhenaten, for the Deutsche Orient-Gesellschaft. On December 6, 1912, he discovered a collection of portraits in a villa that had belonged to the sculptor Thutmose, including more than 20 plaster prototypes and carved stone heads of royal family members. The most famous one is the bust of Queen Nefertiti wearing a tall blue flat-topped crown.

Then, there were those from the archaeologically rich countries of the Mediterranean, such as Ernesto Schiaparelli who headed the Italian Archaeological Mission to Egypt and directed excavations in the Valley of the Queens where many 18th to 20th Dynasty queens, princesses, and princes were buried. In 1904, he discovered the tomb of Nefertari, principal wife of Ramses II. Although plundered in antiquity, the tomb's brilliantly painted stucco reliefs show Nefertari with various deities and texts to ensure her safe passage to the next world. In the 1960s and '70s, another Italian archaeologist, Paolo Matthiae, excavated the extensive 3rd-millennium B.C. Royal Palace of Ebla in Syria. Around the same time, in 1977, Greek excavator Manolis Andronikos discovered the tombs of the ancient royal family of Macedon at the site of Vergina. In recognition of the importance of the find, he later received the Grand Cross of the Order of the Phoenix, Greece's highest honor.

The French also made noteworthy contributions during the early days of archaeology. Egyptologist Pierre Montet studied at the University of Lyon in 1905, and began work at the Institut Français d'Archéologie Orientale in Cairo. But he left Egypt to work in Lebanon from 1921 to 1924, where he found and excavated the 2nd-millennium B.C. royal cemetery of Byblos. Montet returned to Egypt and began digging at Tanis in 1929, but it was only in 1939 that he made his great discovery, the royal necropolis of the 21st and 22nd Dynasty with treasures almost equal to those of Tutankhamun. Jean-Yves Empereur, born in 1952, served at the École Française d'Athènes and worked in Greece, Cyprus, and Turkey, before establishing the Center for Alexandrian Studies. Since then, he has excavated Alexandria's archaeological wealth on land and in the sea. Founded by Alexander the Great in 331 B.C., the city was a commercial and cultural center and capital famous for its library and museum, as well as its lighthouse, one of the Seven Wonders of the Ancient World.

Alberto Ruz Lhuillier, on the other hand, had a more international background. Born in France and educated in Cuba, he later became a Mexican citizen. Ruz will always be remembered for his 1952 discovery of the tomb of K'inich Janaab Pakal, or "Pakal the Great," whose haunting jade death mask ranks among the finest to survive from the ancient world.

To the south, Peruvian archaeologist Walter Alva began unraveling the mysteries of the Moche civilization in the 1980s while working at Sipán in the Lambayeque Valley. In 1978, Russian archaeologist Viktor Sarianidi made a remarkable discovery in war-torn Afghanistan—more than 20,000 gold treasures that had been ensconced in a royal family's tomb for some 2000 years.

Finally, no list of great archaeologists would be complete without Zahi Hawass, who as Head of the Supreme Council for Antiquities has transformed archaeology in Egypt. He has focused on site preservation and museum construction, and upgraded the training and level of expertise in the country, and campaigned vigorously for the return of looted antiquities to Egypt. His own research has included excavation of the tombs of workers at the Giza Plateau, women's roles in ancient Egypt, the late period necropolis at the Bahariyah Oasis (the Valley of the Golden Mummies), and application of DNA analysis to the royal mummies.

While there are sure to be more great archaeologists in the century to come, those on the following pages will always be remembered as among the first to captivate the world's attention and inspire untold generations to unearth our shared past. (EBM)

Layard of Niniveh:
A British Gentleman in Assyria

Although he was a successful British politician and diplomat, Austen Henry Layard (1817–1894) is best known as the excavator of Nimrud. Layard began his professional career working for six years in his uncle's legal office, but he then decided to travel overland to Ceylon (Sri Lanka) where he hoped to obtain a civil service post. He started in 1839, but abandoned the plan after spending several months in Persia.

He returned to Constantinople. From 1842 to 1845, Layard was employed by Sir Stratford Canning, the British ambassador. Canning encouraged him to explore the Assyrian ruins in what is modern-day Iraq, giving him £60 ($89) to support the work.

Layard went to Mosul in 1845 and began excavations first at Nimrud then at Kuyunjik, which he had seen in his earlier travels. At Nimrud, Biblical city of Kalakh and the Assyrian capital, he discovered the palaces of the kings Ashurnasirpal II (883–859 B.C.) and Esarhaddon (681–699 B.C.) in only a few weeks. The walls of Ashurnasirpal's palace were covered with remarkable alabaster reliefs showing the king hunting or at war, protected by winged spirits. At Kuyunjik, where Layard began digging in 1847, he found yet another palace.

Layard returned to England in late 1847. He published the results of his work in *Nineveh and Its Remains* (1848–1849) and *Illustrations of the Monuments of Nineveh* (1849). Despite the titles, these refer mainly to his work at Nimrud (Biblical Kalakh), which Layard took to be a district of Nineveh. He later found evidence that the ruins at Kuyunjik were, in fact, Nineveh. Layard's *Nineveh and Its Remains* became an immediate bestseller, remarkable for its lively writing.

A year later, Layard returned to Constantinople from which, in August 1849, he embarked on a second expedition. This time, he was an official emissary of the British Museum, and the House of Commons funded his work with £3,000 ($4450). Layard resumed excavations at Nimrud and Nineveh. Benefiting from new cuneiform translations by Henry Rawlinson and others, he identi-

fied the "palace without rival" of Sennacherib (704–681 B.C.) at Nineveh, with its wall reliefs, as well as the library of Ashurbanipal with 22,000 cuneiform clay tablets. He also made some soundings during a brief visit to Babylon in 1850 before abandoning the site.

During these expeditions, often in circumstances of great difficulty, Layard sent to England the splendid specimens that now form the greater part of the collection of Assyrian antiquities in the British Museum. In 1847, after discovering several pairs of colossal statues of winged lions and bulls, Layard decided on taking one of each back to London. He accomplished that, but only after several near disasters. His account of lowering a bull, found in its original location and still upright, onto rollers with ropes, pulleys, and levers is horrifying by today's archaeological standards. Especially since Layard says he was forced to use small ropes sent over desert from Aleppo, and a single thick palm fiber cable obtained in Baghdad:

"The men being ready, and all my preparations complete, I stationed myself on top of the high bank of earth over the second bull, and ordered the wedges to be struck out from under the sculpture…. A rope having been passed around it, six or seven men easily tilted it over. The thick, ill-made cable stretched with the strain…. Away went the bull, steady enough as long as supported by the props behind; but as it came nearer to the rollers, the beams could no longer be used. The cable and ropes stretched more and more…they all broke when the sculpture was within four or five feet of the rollers. The bull was precipitated to the ground…. I rushed into the trenches, prepared to find the bull in many pieces. It would be difficult to describe my satisfaction, when I saw it lying precisely where I had wished to place it, and uninjured!"

In 1851, Layard turned his back on fieldwork, vowing never to return to Nineveh. Instead, he turned to politics, being elected to British parliament in the 1850s and 1860s and serving as Under-Secretary for Foreign Affairs. In 1877, he was appointed ambassa-

20 Austen Henry Layard, an English archaeologist, politician, and diplomat, is famous for his excavations
at the Mesopotamian sites of Nimrud and Nineveh.

22-23 and 23 Color drawings done during Layard's excavations in Mesopotamia were used for some
of the archaeologist's publications related to the Assyrian monuments he had discovered (British Museum, London).

Excavations at Nineveh.

dor at Constantinople, where he remained until 1880, when he retired from public life.

Although he no longer took part in excavating, Layard did not quit archaeology completely. He published *A Popular Account of Discoveries at Nineveh* (1852), *Discoveries in the Ruins of Nineveh and Babylon* (1853), and *A Second Series of the Monuments of Nineveh* (1853). His last work, aside from a posthumous autobiography, was *Early Adventures in Persia, Susiana, and Babylonia* (1887). In fact, Layard's legacy is owed not to his skill as an excavator, but to his energy in the field and, especially, to his writing afterward. Still enjoyable to read today, his books brought the Assyrian culture to popular attention, as did the sculptures, cuneiform tablets, and other finds he took to the British Museum. The wholesale removal of antiquities from countries is of course no longer tolerated, but in this Layard must be judged in the light of his own culture and time. (MR)

24-25 This illustration was used for the frontispiece of Layard's book, *Nineveh and Its Remains*. It depicts the complex operation of removing a winged bull the archaeologist found in Nimrud, so that it could be transported. Despite extensive technical difficulties, Layard managed to get many of the objects and monuments discovered throughout his excavations to the British Museum.

25 This winged bull made of stone once decorated the palace of Assyrian King Ashurnasirpal II (883–859 B.C.), in Nimrud. Layard discovered the bull during excavations conducted between 1845 and 1851. It was then transported to England (British Museum, London).

26 This sketch by Layard depicts a relief that the English archaeologist discovered in the palace of Ashurnasirpal II, in Nimrud. Winged supernatural beings like those shown here were often placed at entrances for protection, and are referred to as *apkallu* in cuneiform texts.

27 This winged genie from the palace of Ashurnasirpal II, in Nimrud, holds a pinecone in one hand and a woven pouch in the other (Louvre Museum, Paris).

28-29 and 29   In 1846, Layard found this relief among the ruins of the Ashurnasirpal II palace in Nimrud. It depicts an Assyrian military encampment from an unusual aerial perspective. The inner section is divided into four quarters with scenes of food preparation and cooking. To the right of the encampment, some horses are drinking water while a soldier inspects another horse inside a pen. On the far right, an official notes the arrival of a few prisoners (below), while (above) a soldier faces two leonine figures (British Museum, London).

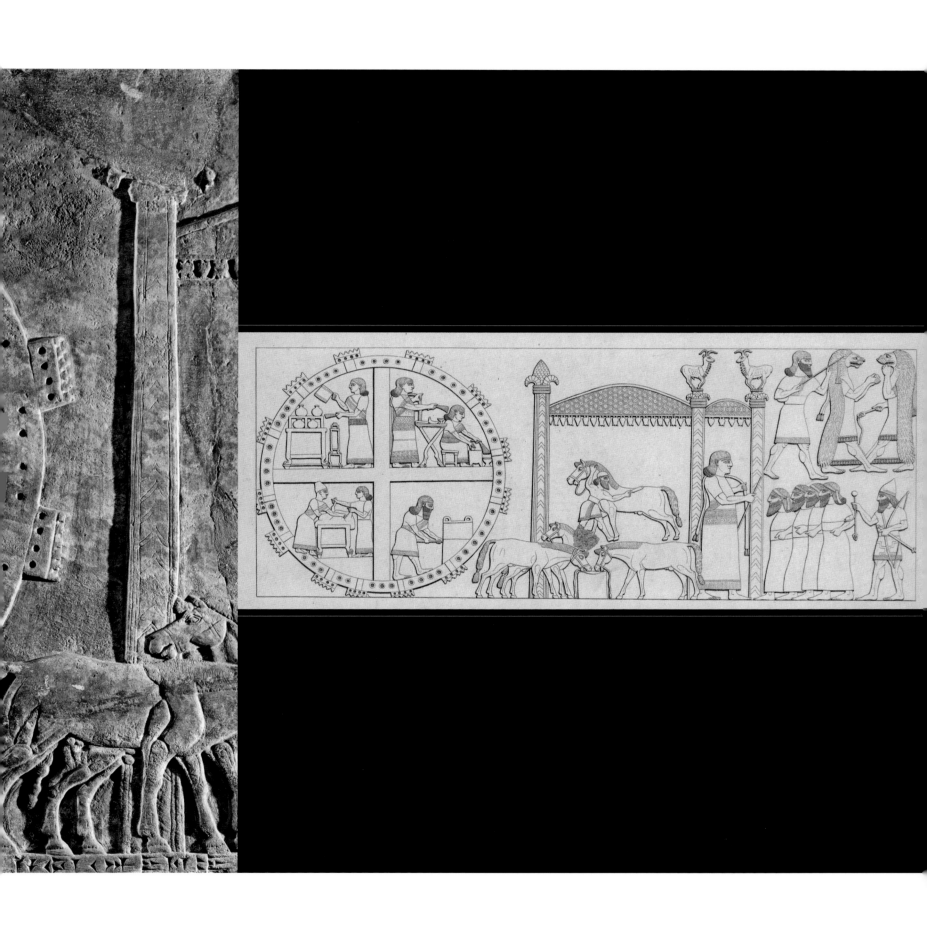

30 and 31 Discovered by
Layard among the Temple
of Ishtar ruins in Nimrud,
this magnesite statue
depicts the Assyrian king
Ashurnasirpal II. The ruler
holds a mace and a sickle,
symbols of his power.
Cuneiform text on his
chest reveals his name and
title. A drawing of the
statue (on right) was
published in Layard's 1853
book, *A Second Series of
the Monuments of
Nineveh* (British Museum,
London).

32-33 A drawing of a
colossal lion statue found
among the Temple of
Ishtar ruins in Nimrud was
published in Layard's *A
Second Series of the
Monuments of Nineveh*
(1853). Layard brought the
statue to England, and
today it can be found at
the British Museum.

34-35 Scenes of a king
hunting lions in his military
chariot are a common
theme in Assyrian
iconography. In this relief
from Nimrud, the king is
Ashurnasirpal II (British
Museum, London).

Plate 52. Entire Statue from the North West ruins. (Nimroud.)

Plate I. Sessal Li

reat Entrance (Nimroud.)

In the Footsteps of Homer:
Heinrich Schliemann

"It seems," wrote Heinrich Schliemann of his excavation at Troy, "that Divine Providence has brilliantly recompensed me for my superhuman efforts during my three years of excavation." Schliemann is one of archaeology's most controversial figures, accounted by some a fraud, by others a pioneer. Schliemann claimed to have received a copy of Georg Ludwig Jerrer's *Universal History* as a present when he was eight years old and that pictures of Troy in it inspired him. "Father! I answered, if such walls once existed they cannot have been completely destroyed: vast ruins of them must still remain, but hidden away beneath the dust of ages.... In the end we both agreed that I should one day excavate Troy." That is the story—a young boy captivated by the legend of Troy and determined to grow up and prove Homer right. But the truth is that Schliemann's decision to excavate Troy came much later, in 1868 at age 46.

It is clear that Schliemann "enhanced" his personal history shamelessly, for example by borrowing from other sources. His "eyewitness" account of a fire in San Francisco in 1851 was likely copied from a newspaper, and his tale of fending off four attacking dogs in Greece was taken from a guidebook. Other cases are more than just romanticizing. He fraudulently obtained U.S. citizenship in 1869, then immediately—and illegally—divorced his first wife.

The critical question is to what extent his fictions might have contaminated his archaeological work. Schliemann took credit for the ideas of others, notably Frank Calvert who realized that Hissarlik, a mound partly on his property in northwest Anatolia was ancient Troy. He lied about finding inscriptions in the backyard of his house in Athens and a bust of Cleopatra at Alexandria. In his published reports Schliemann sometimes said objects found at different times and places were part of the same discovery.

Born January 6, 1822, Schliemann left his native Germany when he was 19, boarded a ship bound for Colombia that, however, became stranded on the coast of Holland by a storm. Schliemann moved to Amsterdam where he worked as a clerk. In 1844, he began working for the B.H. Schröder and Co. trading house, which soon sent him to St. Petersburg as a commodities trading agent. Schliemann started his own agency, dealing in indigo and other goods and accumulating a great personal fortune. In 1866 and 1867, he took archaeology course at the Sorbonne in Paris. After divorcing his first wife, Schliemann, then 47, married the 17-year-old Sophia Engastroménos, who he selected from photographs of prospective brides sent to him by the Archbishop of Mantinea, his old ancient Greek tutor.

Equipped with the Homeric epics as guidebooks, and funded by his vast wealth, Schliemann began looking for Troy. Between 1870 and 1873, he unearthed large portions of an ancient citadel at Hissarlik, with sloping stone walls that matched, after a fashion, the description in the *Iliad*. Schliemann's discovery of Troy brought him worldwide fame and silenced some of his critics, scholars who looked down on him as a poorly trained amateur.

It was in the in the spring of 1873 that Schliemann make his greatest find at Troy, a cache of bronze and gold vessels, weapons, and jewelry that he called "Priam's Treasure" after the Trojan king in the *Iliad*. But the treasure is haunted by many of the questions that surround Schliemann's honesty. David Traill, who has studied the diaries and correspondence of Schliemann, concludes that a major find was made on May 31, 1873. Weeks later, Schliemann wrote, "It would, however, have been impossible for me to have removed the Treasure without the help of my dear wife, who stood by me ready to pack the things which I cut out in her shawl." But he confessed to Sir Charles Newton of the British Museum that Sophia had actually left the site in early May but "since I am endeavoring to make an archaeologist of her, I wrote in my book that she had been present and assisted me in taking out the treasure." Schliemann's Greek foreman Nikolaos Zaphyros Yannakis was likely the one who helped him dig out the treasure.

36 After various jobs in trade and commerce around the world, Heinrich Schliemann finally decided to take up archaeology in 1868. The profession would make him famous worldwide.

37 top This 1875 photograph shows the huts in the field where Schliemann was excavating, around the hill of Hissarlik.

37 bottom The team of workers posed on the city wall were led by Wilhelm Dörpfeld, Schliemann's partner and successor in the excavations at Troy.

38 The great walls of Troy are pictured here, during excavations in 1893.

But it is uncertain exactly what was in the find originally. Schliemann smuggled it to Greece, under the eyes of the Ottoman authorities. It is possible that he added to it pieces that he had found earlier, removing them as a single group. In Book 24 of the *Iliad*, Homer describes treasure brought by Priam to Achilles as ransom for the body of Hector: robes of state, cloaks, rugs, capes of snowy linen, bars of gold, tripods, cauldrons, and more. Schliemann was not above adding to the find to make it as impressive as the treasure described by Homer.

Schliemann's hope that he had found Priam's Treasure was unfounded. He uncovered remains of nine major levels at Troy. The Treasure came not from the end of the Late Bronze Age, about the time a historical Trojan War might have occurred, but from an Early Bronze Age fortification wall circa 2200 B.C., a millennium earlier than the period in which Priam would have lived, if he ever lived at all.

Schliemann worked at a pivotal time in archaeology. His later excavation at Troy, guide in part by Wilhelm Dörpfeld, reflected the future of the field. Credit is due Schliemann for some specific fine points, such as having animal remains from the site examined by experts, but his achievement is on a larger scale, as the father of Aegean prehistory, both brilliant and deeply flawed. (MR)

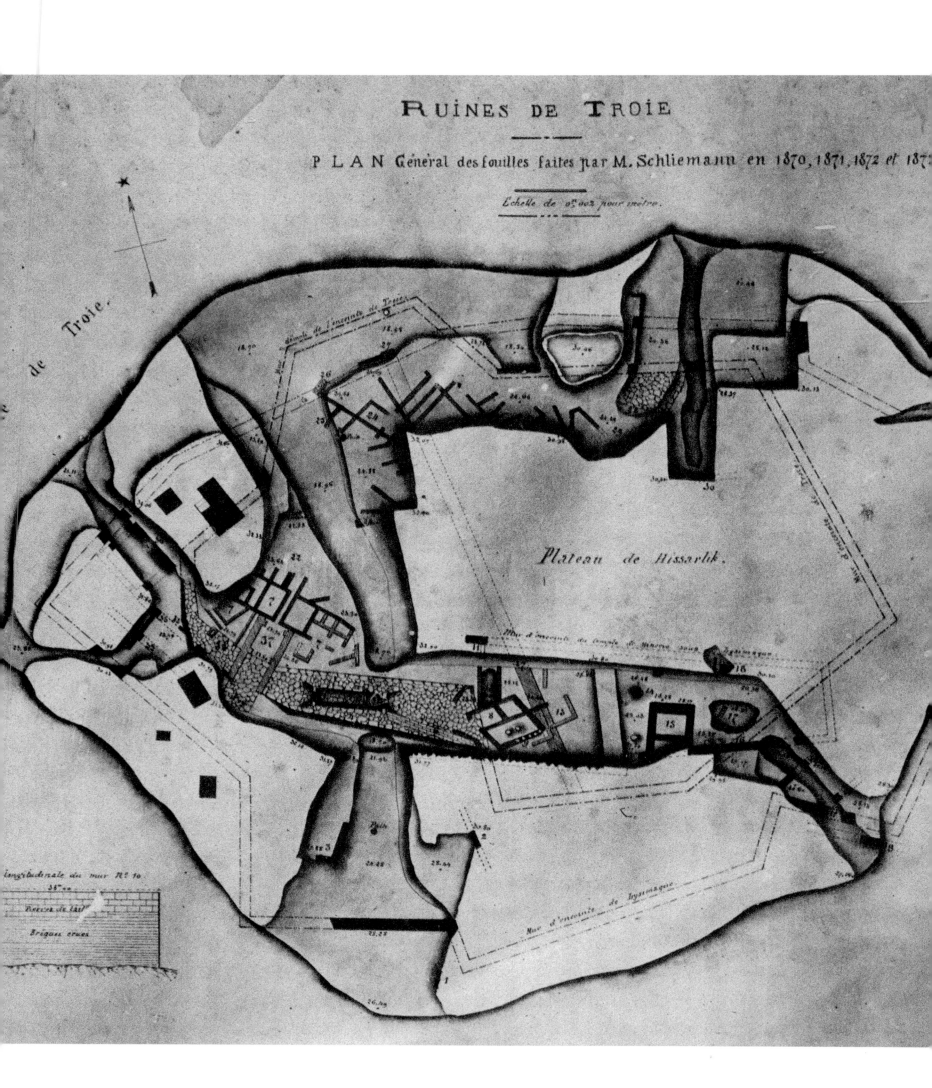

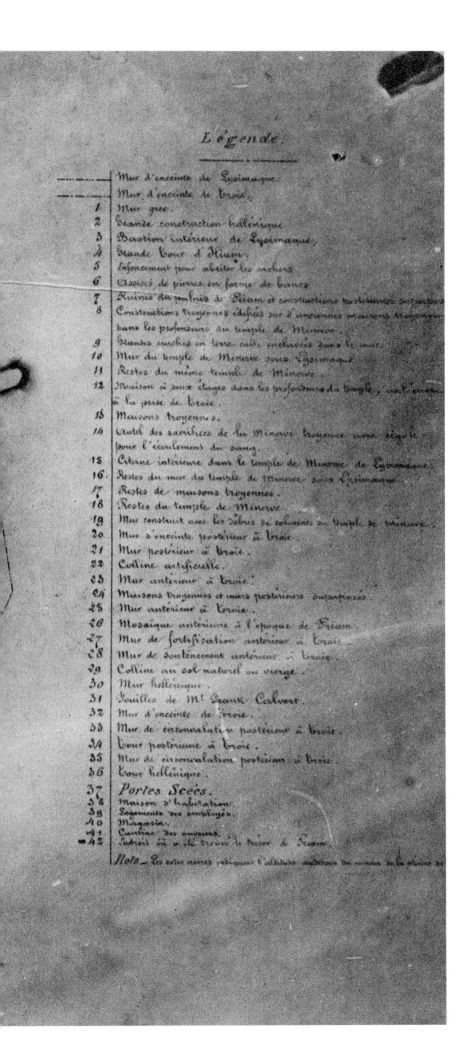

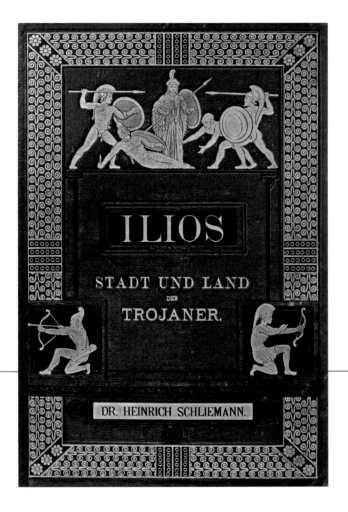

40-41 This map shows the position of ruins uncovered in Troy, following Schliemann's excavations between 1870 and 1873. It was published in *Trojanischer Alterthümer (Troy and Its Remains)* in 1874.

41 In 1881, Schliemann published *Ilios: Stadt und Land der Trojaner (Ilios: The City and Country of the Trojans)* chronicling the results of his excavations in the city immortalized by Homer.

42 and 43 Schliemann found the cache known as Priam's Treasure on May 31, 1873. Located at the "Troy II" level and dating back to the middle of the 3rd millennium B.C., it included a copper shield and cauldron, metallic cups and vases, copper weapons, and magnificent gold jewelry known as the Jewels of Helen. A photograph taken in 1880 (left) shows the entire treasure, before it was divided among the Istanbul and Berlin collections. A double-spouted gold sauceboat (right) was part of the treasure (Pushkin Museum, Moscow).

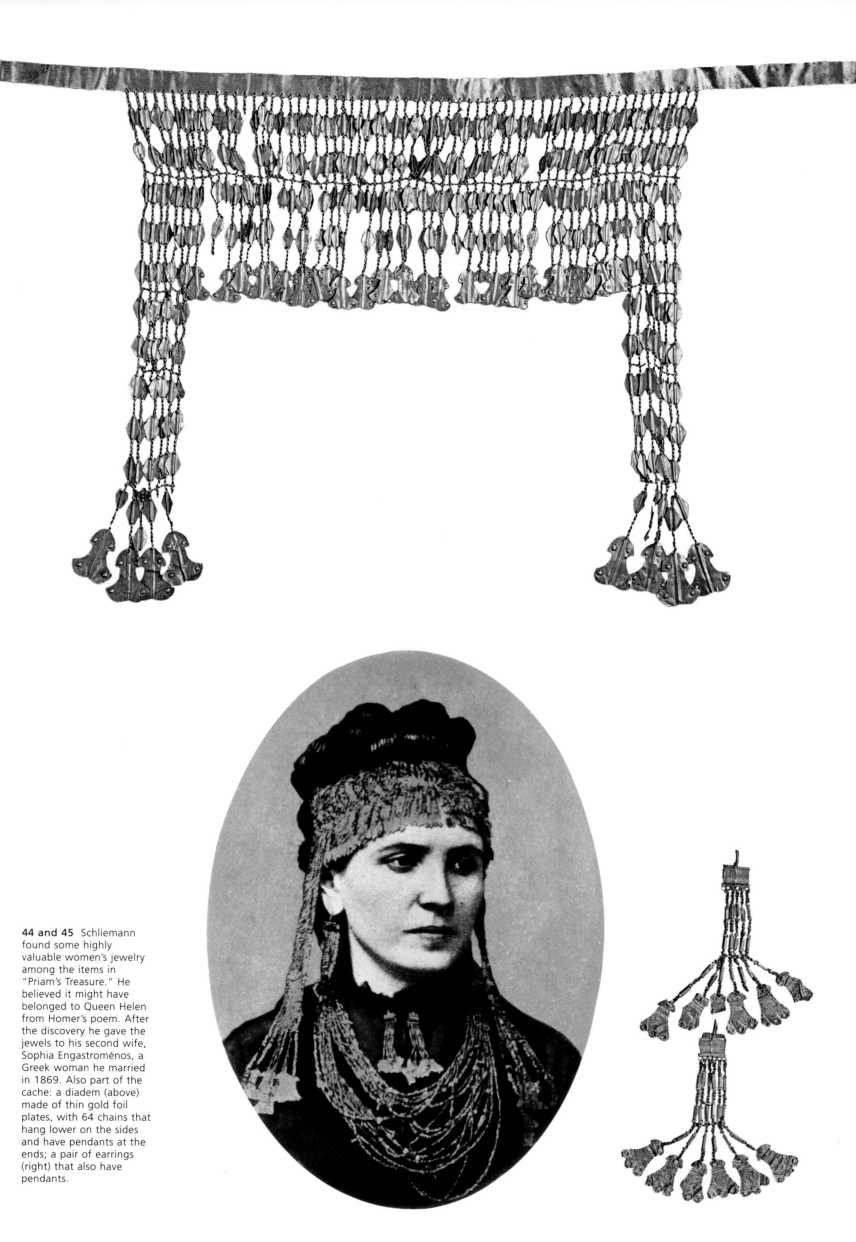

44 and 45 Schliemann found some highly valuable women's jewelry among the items in "Priam's Treasure." He believed it might have belonged to Queen Helen from Homer's poem. After the discovery he gave the jewels to his second wife, Sophia Engastroménos, a Greek woman he married in 1869. Also part of the cache: a diadem (above) made of thin gold foil plates, with 64 chains that hang lower on the sides and have pendants at the ends; a pair of earrings (right) that also have pendants.

PLATE XIX.

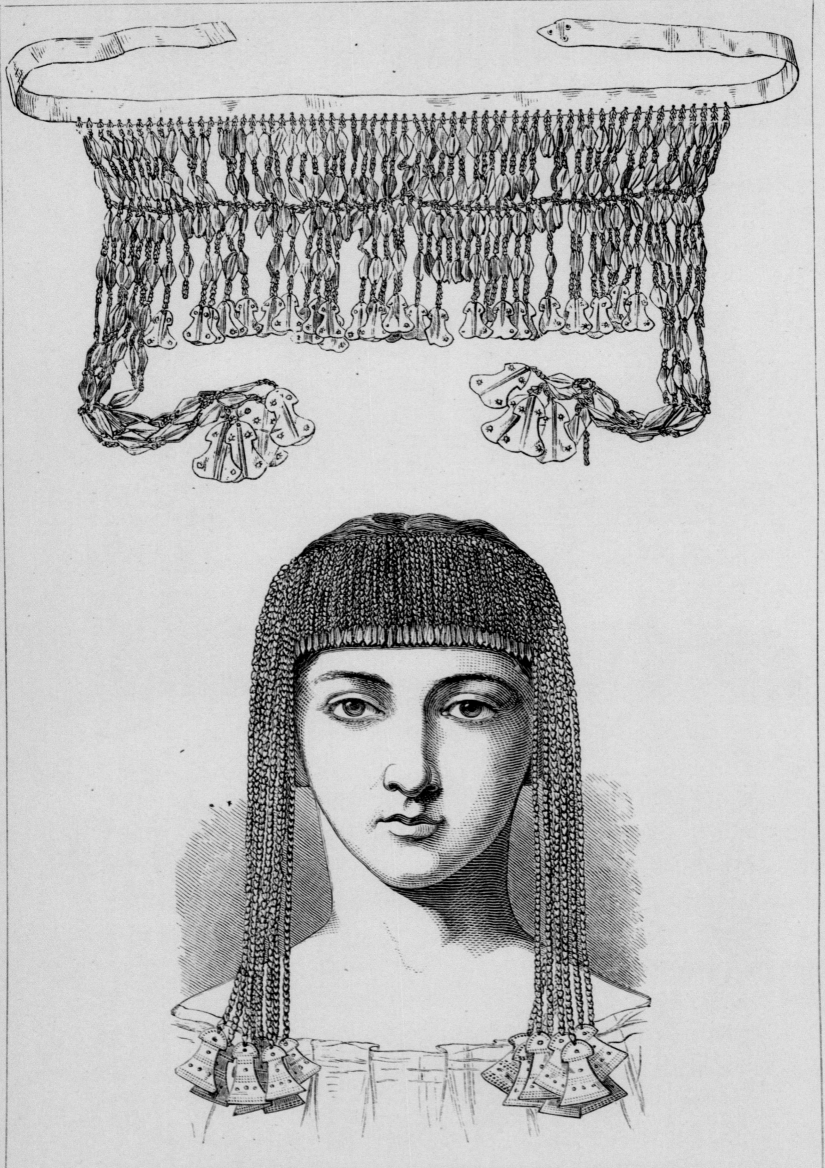

Nos. 276 and 277.—The two Golden Diadems (πλεκταί ἀναδέσμαι).

THE TREASURE OF PRIAM. *Page* 335.

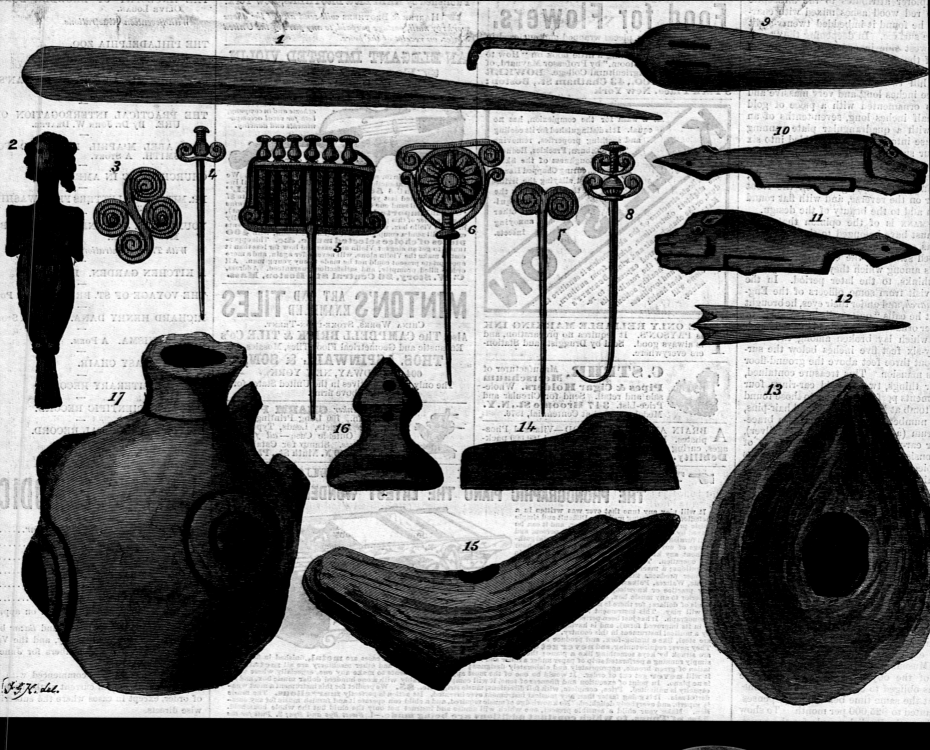

46 top In addition to gold jewelry, there were also weapons and instruments made of ivory, bone, and clay among the items Schliemann found in Troy.

46 bottom This bead from a necklace, part of Priam's Treasure, consists of four spirals made from thin gold foil (Pushkin Museum, Moscow).

47 top This gold pin, one of the pieces found in Priam's Treasure, is characterized by spiral shapes with miniature vases resting on top (Pushkin Museum, Moscow).

47 bottom This pin from Priam's Treasure is decorated in a floral motif with side openings and was probably made by the same goldsmith as the previous one (Pushkin Museum, Moscow).

Schliemann at Mycenae:
The Tombs of the Atreidai

Having "discovered" Troy and unearthed "Priam's Treasure" there, Schliemann turned his attention to Mycenae, a Late Bronze Age city and fortress, at the head of the Gulf of Argos on the southern Greek mainland. According to Homer, Mycenae was the home of Agamemnon, the leader of the Greeks at Troy and the brother of Menelaus, whose wife Helen ran away with the Trojan prince Paris, sparking the war.

Vestiges of Mycenae were visible throughout antiquity, from the Lion Gate, so named for its sculptures, to vast beehive- shaped tombs identified by the ancient geographer Pausanias as those of Agamemnon, his followers, and members of the royal house. A reconnaissance in 1874 was promising, and Schliemann began excavating at Mycenae in earnest in the fall of 1876 on behalf of the Greek Archaeological Society.

Working within the main citadel wall, just inside the Lion Gate, Schliemann's men unearthed stelai around the perimeter of a 90-ft (28-m) circle in which were five "shaft graves" cut deeply into the earth. By the end of November he had excavated tombs containing the bodies of several Mycenaean rulers, five of whom were buried with gold face masks. Elated, Schliemann sent a telegram to King George of Greece: "With great joy I announce to Your Majesty that I have discovered the tombs which the tradition proclaimed by Pausanias indicates to be the graves of Agamemnon, Cassandra, Eurymedon and their companions, all slain at a banquet by Clytemnestra and her lover Aegisthos." With the burials were gold decorations; bronze weapons, some with gold hilts and inlaid blades, gold and silver cups, ivory containers, and amber beads.

As at Troy, however, there were serious problems with Schliemann's interpretations at Mycenae. He wrote:

"For my part, I have always firmly believed in the Trojan War; my full faith in the tradition has never been shaken by mode and criticism, and to this faith of mine I am indebted for the discovery of Troy and its treasure…. My firm faith in the traditions made me undertake my late excavations in the acropolis [of Mycenae] and led to the discovery of the five tombs with their immense treasures… I have not the slightest objection to admitting that the tradition which assigns the tombs to Agamemnon and his companions may be perfectly correct."

It is now known that the shaft graves were some 300 years earlier than the supposed date of the Trojan War, so no connection can be made between the remains in them and the characters immortalized by Homer.

Other disagreements exist concerning specific objects Schliemann says were found in the grave circle. For example, there are two Late Helladic (LH III B) terracotta figurines from Shaft Grave 1, but they date several centuries later than the grave. Pottery said to be from Grave 1 appears to have actually been found on the acropolis on November 15, according to Schliemann's diary.

The most worrisome concerns are centered on the so-called "Mask of Agamemnon." Of all the gold and electrum funerary masks discovered at the site, it is the most famous. "I have gazed on the face of Agamemnon," Schliemann is said to have telegrammed a Greek newspaper on first seeing the mask. In fact, he himself never identified it as belonging to Agamemnon, but since it was the finest one it became associated with the hero. Nor did Schliemann ever note in writing the obvious stylistic differences—facial hair, ears cut out from the body of the mask—that set it apart from all of the others. Some scholars today suspect that it might be a fake, planted by Schliemann to augment the genuine finds, or possibly is an original that was modified to look more lordly (for example the mustache and beard, which are more in accord with those of late-19th-century styles among the nobility than with features on the other masks from Mycenae).

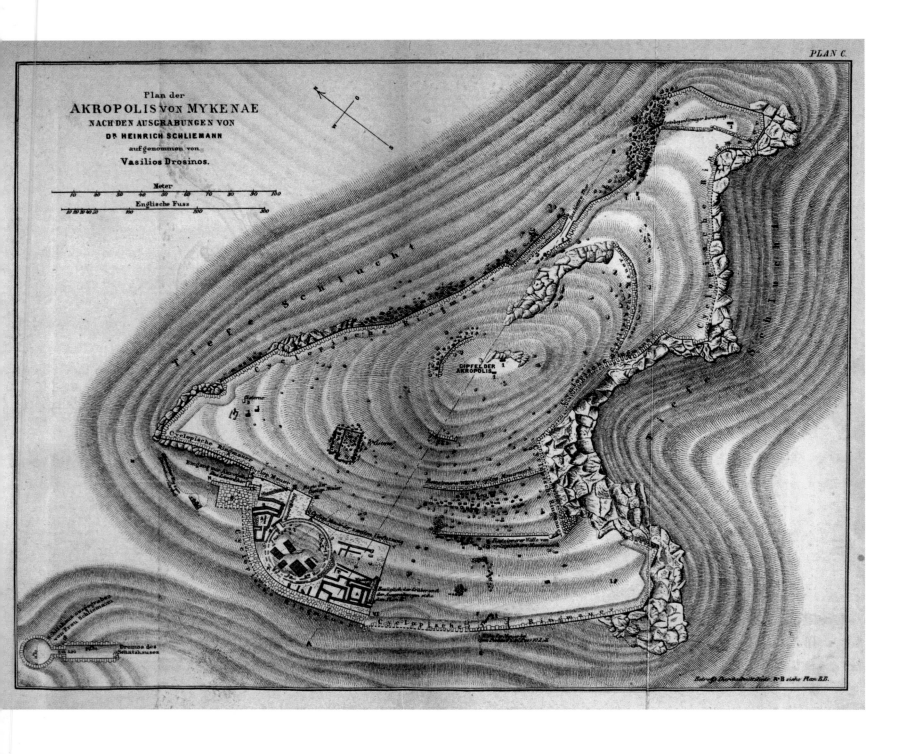

48 The Lion Gate marks
the entrance to the fortress
of Mycenae. A stone slab
above the gate depicts a
carving of two lionesses,
one on each side of
a column.

50 This 1878 plan of the
Mycenae fortress shows the
structures uncovered by
Schliemann.

51 An extension of the
fortress wall at Mycenae
included Grave Circle A.

The masks and gold jewelry Schliemann found at Mycenae brought him world fame; he was henceforth known as the father of Mycenaean archaeology. Clearly that is an overstatement. Credit for success of the work at Mycenae belongs also to Schliemann's aid Wilhelm Dörpfeld and Panagiotis Stamatakis, the official representative of the Greek Archaeological Service, who devised a system of classification of finds at the site, and made certain that remains of later periods, including Roman, were recorded before Schliemann removed them in his search for Homer's Mycenae. (MR)

52-53 and 53 Grave Circle A is within the most recent enclosure wall of Mycenae and contains six royal tombs. Schliemann found various objects inside, such as bronze swords, jewelry, pottery, and the famous gold masks. News of the German archaeologist's discoveries spread, and by the late 19th century Mycenae had already become a tourist attraction.

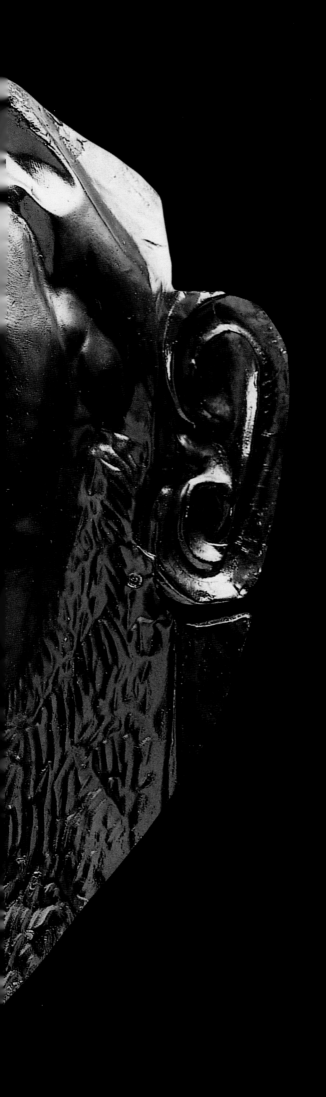

54-55 Found in Tomb V of Grave Circle A in Mycenae, this is popularly known as the "Mask of Agamemnon." The splendid gold mask depicts the likeness of an elderly Mycenaean prince. Some scholars suggest Schliemann altered it to make it appear more kingly (National Archaeological Museum, Athens).

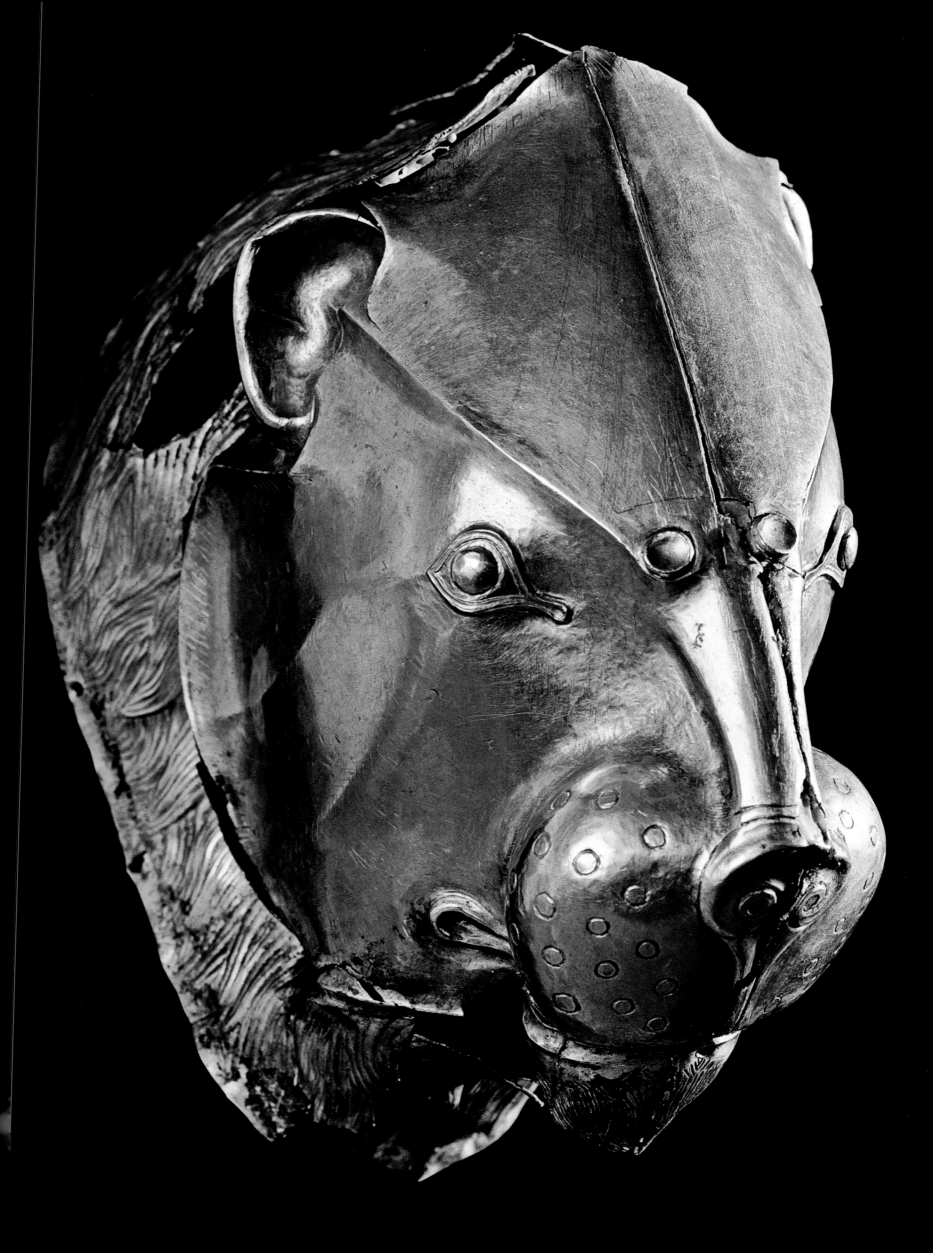

56 Schliemann found this gold rhyton (libation cup), which depicts a lion head, in Tomb IV of Grave Circle A in Mycenae (National Archaeological Museum, Athens).

57 Three male bodies were buried in Tomb V of Grave Circle A in Mycenae, where Schliemann found this gold pectoral with a spiral motif in 1876 (National Archaeological Museum, Athens).

Robert Koldewey:
An Architect in Babylon

Between 1899 and 1917, German archaeologist and architect Robert Koldewey unearthed the famous ancient city of Babylon in Iraq. One of his most remarkable discoveries at the site was the foundation of a ziggurat, or stepped tower, on top of which the temple of the city-god Marduk once stood. Many associate it with the Biblical Tower of Babel, also called Etemenanki, where according to the Book of Genesis, the structure was built under the ruler Nimrod to soar to great heights into the heavens. Instead of being used as a place of worship, however, it was celebrated as an achievement of man. This angered the Hebrew god Yahweh so deeply that he expelled its builders to all corners of the earth, and punished them by limiting their ability to communicate with each other—forcing them to speak different languages.

While popular depictions of the Biblical Tower of Babel, including a famous painting by Netherlandish artist Pieter Brueghel the Elder, show a massive circular structure, Koldewey found the foundations of a square zigurrat. Not much remains of the tower, except for fragments of three stairs that once led up to it. He also excavated the more well-preserved Processional Way that led up to it from Babylon's palace and inner town, where the so-called "Ishtar Gate" once stood. The massive, arched gate—built by Nebuchadnezzar II who ruled from 604 to 562 B.C.—is made of glazed mud bricks, whose decorated surface, in raised relief, depicts yellow bulls and white dragons, the latter of which were sacred to Marduk, against a cerulean background. The Processional Way was also decorated with colorful glazed bricks showing striding lions, which are associated with Ishtar, goddess of love and war. Scholars argue that these lions were meant to "protect" the street.

Koldewey also excavated 14 large rooms with arched stone ceilings in the basement of the site's Southern Citadel, which led him to believe he had unearthed the area under which the legendary man-made Hanging Gardens of Babylon once stood. (Ancient texts had noted that stone was used in only two places in the city—the north wall of the Northern Citadel and in the Hanging Gardens.) Regarded today as one of the Seven Wonders of the Ancient World, the Hanging Gardens were built by the ruler Nebuchadnezzar II for his wife, Amyitis, daughter of the king of the Medes who longed for the lush plants and trees of her native land while she lived in the unforgiving desert city of Babylon in Mesopotamia. Current scholarship, however, disputes Koldewey's claim for lack of any further substantiating evidence, and the location of the Hanging Gardens of Babylon remains a mystery.

Koldewey also participated in excavations in Greece and Turkey. He worked during the nascent years of "modern" archaeology, and is often credited with more than just his great discoveries—he is highly regarded for having incorporated sound methodology and newly developed excavation techniques at a very early time. According to a September 5, 1915, *New York Times* book review of Koldewey's *Excavations at Babylon*:

"Excavation is nowadays something more than a mere art; it might almost be described as an exact science. By careful measurements and meticulous preservation of relics the modern explorer wrings its secrets out of the most difficult site . . . [I]t is remarkable how much [Koldewey] has already uncovered and how ingeniously he has determined the character of the different buildings and roads which have thus yielded their secrets to the spades of his workmen."

Although many important structures at the site still stand, Babylon was heavily damaged both by Saddam Hussein and by military campaigns during the recent war in Iraq. (EBM)

58 Babylon's famous Processional Way was decorated with striding lions, which were associated with Ishtar, the goddess of love and war (Vorderasiatisches Museum, Berlin).

60 top Excavator Robert Koldewey was well equipped to deal with the site's complicated monuments, as he had just spent a decade teaching architecture in Görlitz, Germany.

60 bottom In the late 1920s, Koldewey had the entire Ishtar Gate shipped brick by brick to his native Germany, where it was reassembled—and now stands—in Berlin's Vorderasiatisches Museum.

60-61 Built during the reign of Nebuchadnezzar II, the Ishtar Gate was excavated by Koldewey between 1902 and 1914.

62-63 and 64-65 The Ishtar Gate once stood at the entrance to Babylon's inner town. Participants in religious ceremonies would have passed through it as they traveled along the Processional Way to the most sacred inner temple. The gate is decorated with brightly colored glazed bricks that depict in relief dragons and bulls, which were sacred to the gods (Vorderasiatisches Museum, Berlin).

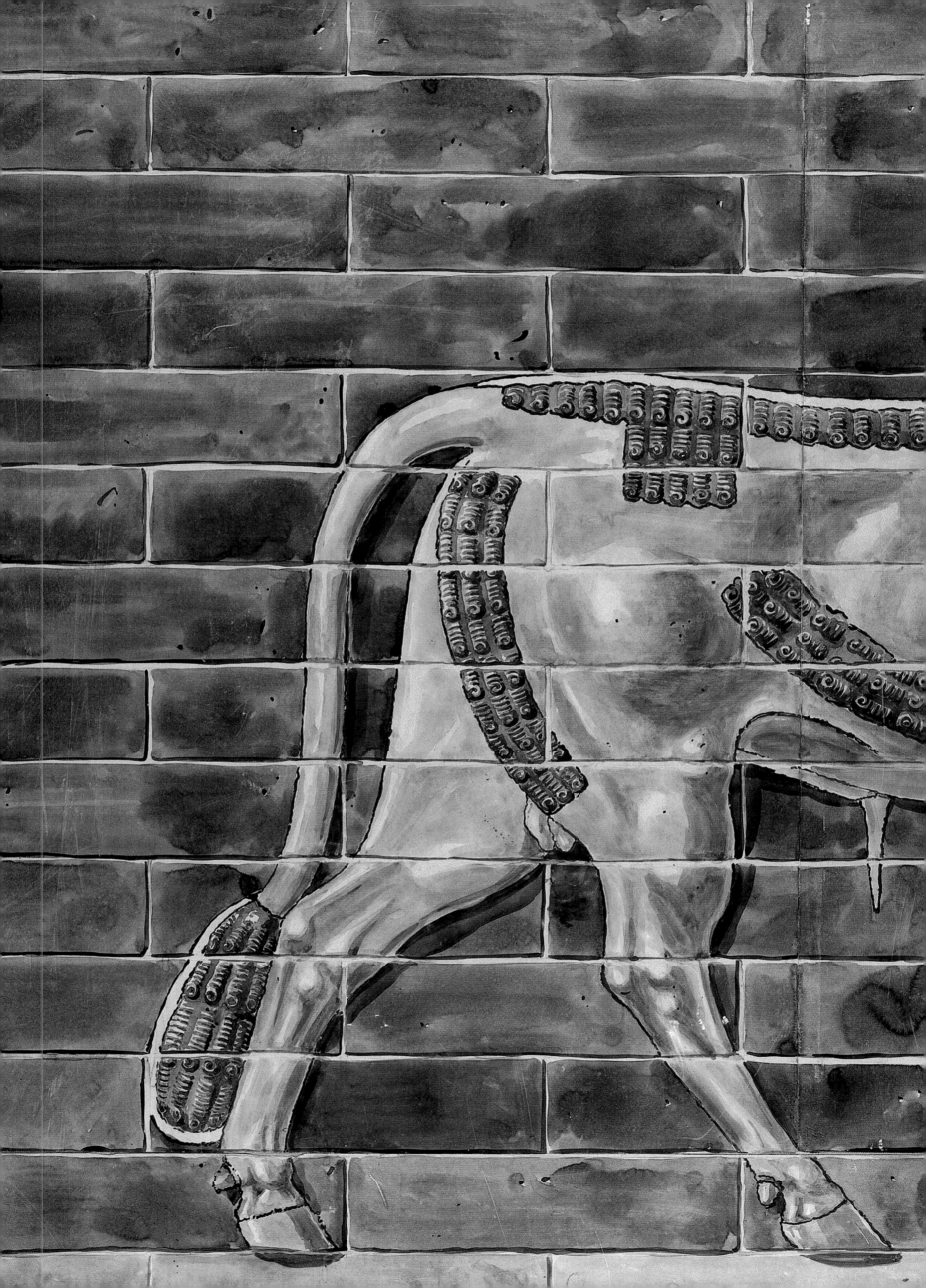

Arthur Evans:
In the Minotaur's Labyrinth

The Greek Bronze Age civilization of the Minoans (3100–1050 B.C.) first came to light under the trowel of British archaeologist Arthur Evans on the island of Crete in the early 20th century. Excavating a five-acre plot of land he had purchased in 1900, he discovered the remains of a sprawling building whose storage magazines formed a mazelike pattern. The distinct architecture inspired Evans to claim he had unearthed the labyrinth of the part-man part-bull Minotaur, the mythical creature that had devoured Athenian children sent as tribute to Crete's King Minos. According to legend, Theseus, one of the Athenians sent as a sacrificial victim to appease the Minotaur, instead slew the creature and found his way out of its lair thanks to the king's love-struck daughter, Ariadne.

Evans, however, had uncovered much more than a myth. The complex civilization, which he dubbed "Minoan" after its King Minos, produced fantastic works of art. The interior walls of Knossos were decorated with colorful wall paintings of birds, dolphins, and monkeys, as well as craggy landscapes filled with flowers, and men and women engaged in sacred rituals such as bull-leaping, which involved grabbing the beast's horns to catapult over its back. Excavations showed that this multistory complex, which Evans called a palace, was actually the island's main administrative and distribution center for massive quantities of goods, including olive oil, wine, and grains, as listed on clay tablets in extensive archives. Evans quickly learned that Minoan palatial architecture was extraordinarily advanced, featuring colonnaded courtyards, sliding doors, running water, external staircases, and wooden beams that helped brace the monumental structures from the shock of earthquakes.

Other artifacts excavated at Knossos speak to the skill of its craftsmen, who created jewelry, statuettes, and religious symbols, such as double axes, from gold, silver, ivory, faience, and semi-precious stones. Evans also discovered that the Minoans produced a wide variety of pottery, including handheld conical cups, rhyta from which they poured libations to the gods, and gigantic storage jars. The smaller pieces were often richly decorated. One distinctive type, the "marine style," depicts playful yet amazingly realistic octopi and other marine life, along with coral and shells, signs of the Minoans' intimate connection with the sea. Subsequent excavations throughout Crete have shown that the Minoans were great seafarers who opened trade routes with the powerful kingdoms of Egypt, Anatolia, and the Levant.

Knighted in 1911 for his contributions to the field of archaeology, Evans developed a colorful vocabulary for the nascent study of the Minoans, describing sunken stone chambers as "lustral basins," depictions of bulls' horns as "horns of consecration," and the architecture as "palatial." Archaeologists still fondly employ these terms to this day.

Evans's other lasting legacies are his wild—and in many cases, wildly inaccurate—reconstructions. Today, Knossos is a heap of reinforced concrete with replicas of frescoes hung where they looked best, rather than where they were actually found. The most authentic room is the so-called "Throne Room," where a stone chair with a wavy back and legs carved in relief is still attached to part of its original wall, offering a glimpse at its ancient appearance. The throne is flanked by wall paintings of griffins, mythical creatures with the wings and head of a bird affixed to the body of a lion. Earthy red and white horizontal wavy lines set the griffins in an unearthly landscape. Tantalizingly facing the throne is a lustral basin.

Evans famously took liberties when piecing together many of the spectacular finds from the palace. For example, his reconstructed "Priest-King" fresco shows a man with flowing black hair and an elaborate plumed headdress, or crown, wearing nothing

66 The father of Minoan archaeology, Sir Arthur Evans was the first to come up with a chronology of the great Bronze Age civilization, which he divided into Early, Middle, and Late Minoan periods, based on his excavations at Knossos. A bronze bust of the excavator at the entrance to the site welcomes visitors to this day.

68-69 Minoan palace architecture featured sun-drenched open courtyards. Shown here is the great propylaea, or gateway, which is located at the site's south entrance.

69 Liquid libations for the gods were poured from this magnificent steatite rhyton in the shape of a bull's head, featuring eyes of rock crystal, gilded horns, and a muzzle inlaid with mother of pearl (Iraklion Archaeological Museum).

but a blue codpiece and a striped miniskirt, marching as if in a procession, his right fist placed over his heart. One of the most recognizable images from the palace, the figure was imaginatively reconstructed from just a few fragments of three, perhaps four different scenes. The headdress was found in another room.

With the discovery of the palace of Knossos—and the romantic tale that accompanied it—Evans ignited the public's imagination and has inspired archaeologists for more than a century to delve into the study of Bronze Age Crete. Despite his fanciful reconstructions, Sir Arthur Evans will always be remembered as the father of Minoan archaeology. The generations of archaeologists who succeeded him quickly discovered that the reality of the Minoan civilization was even more fascinating than the myths that surround it. (EBM)

70 The walls of Knossos were richly decorated with colorful paintings depicting scenes from everyday life and nature. This replica features octopus tentacles, which reflects the Minoans' intimate connection with the sea.

71 The Knossos wall paintings also show religious ceremonies. This example (a replica) of a slender young man in profile illustrates one of several "Cup Bearers" from the so-called "Procession fresco."

72 Bulls played a significant role in Minoan religious ceremonies. Shown here is a replica of a wall painting that features a animated bull in relief.

73 top The replica painting of the bull shown at left is featured on the second story of this structure behind distinctively shaped Minoan pillars, also replicas, at the north entrance to the palace.

73 bottom Evans took artistic license as he heavily reconstructed Knossos out of reinforced concrete. Throughout the palace, as here on the Throne Room exterior, he used a different color around the doorframes to represent the wood that originally would have been used there to cushion the stone structure in the event of an earthquake.

74 and 75 Composite bird-lion creatures known as griffins, such as this reconstructed example, were common motifs in the art of the eastern Mediterranean. Believed to be omnipotent, griffins were often associated with the iconography of great rulers. Here, they flank the alabaster "throne"—original to the palace—that faces a lustral basin, or sunken chamber, which may once have been filled with water for purification rituals.

76-77 Minoan bull-leaping was incorporated into rites of passage ceremonies in which young men would grab the horns of the beast and catapult over its back. In this scene, the leaper is assisted by two figures, who may represent young women (Iraklion Archaeological Museum).

Leonard Woolley:
The City of Ur of the Chaldeans

English archaeologist Charles Leonard Woolley (1880–1960) began excavating on a small hill on the southern plain of Iraq, near the Euphrates River, the same year that Howard Carter found Tutankhamun's tomb: 1922. Back in the mid-19th century, the place had already been suggested as the probable location of the remains of the Sumerian city of Ur, cited in the Bible as Abraham's birthplace, but no archaeological exploration had been done.

The mission directed by Woolley was organized by the British Museum in conjunction with the University of Pennsylvania. In addition to the simple search for treasures, they arranged for the systematic scientific study of the site, embodying the new archaeological approach that was coming to life in the early 20th century. Stratigraphic excavation conducted by Woolley's team between 1922 and 1927 allowed them to study the various layers of inhabitation, and it was revealed that the city had been occupied since the beginning of the 4th millennium B.C. This era corresponds to the layer where the archaeologist believed he'd located evidence of the "worldwide flood." After passing through various historical periods (Sumerian, Babylonian, Assyrian, Persian), the city was finally abandoned when the course of the Euphrates River changed, leaving it dry around 400 B.C.

One of the major structures discovered during excavations was the great ziggurat, a brick step pyramid built by the Neo-Sumerian king Ur-Nammu as a shrine to the god Nanna around 2000 B.C., and restored in the Neo-Babylonian era. But Woolley's excavations in the Ur necropolis from 1927 to 1934 yielded the best results: more than 2,000 graves were uncovered. Woolley identified 16 royal tombs among them, two of which were found intact. The tombs of Queen Puabi, King Meskalamdug, and King Abargi contained marvelous gold artifacts: diadems,

rings, jewels, a golden helmet, daggers, statues, vases, and extraordinary musical instruments, like lyres covered in gold leaf. The famous Standard of Ur, a box with mosaics of lapis lazuli, red stone, and shells decorating the sides, also came from one of the necropolis tombs. The depictions on the item provide a vivid representation of Sumerian life, both military and civilian, with the king at the top of the social hierarchy. One particular detail really stood out to archaeologists: there was a pit in every royal tomb with human and animal remains. One contained the remains of 74 people, and was christened the "Great Death Pit." They were lined up in an orderly fashion along the walls of the chamber, one next to the other. Some of these individuals, mostly female, were accompanied by cups and jars as though they had consumed a funeral feast before dying. The skeletons, both male and female, showed no signs of violence. Woolley hypothesized that servants, nobles, or members of the royal family were voluntarily sacrificed, or committed suicide at the moment their ruler died so they might have the honor of being buried near him. Recent investigations by the University of Pennsylvania have used computerized tomography on some of the human remains recovered by Woolley, demonstrating that the individuals were probably killed with a violent blow to the head.

To recover and preserve the fragile objects found in the necropolis, Woolley adopted a method as simple as it was genius: he poured wax over the artifacts and removed them together with the surrounding earth so they could be subsequently uncovered and studied in the laboratory.

Various famous personalities of the era came to visit the important Mesopotamian site throughout the years Woolley spent working at Ur, including King Albert I of Belgium and T.E. Lawrence (Lawrence of Arabia), who had excavated with Woolley in Kharkhemish prior to World War I. Celebrated writer

78 At the end of the excavation season in Ur (1933–1934), Charles Leonard Woolley worked on clearing out Pit X, located in the necropolis that dates to the time of Jemdet Nasr. It took 150 workers to remove 459,000 cubic feet (13,000 cubic meters) of earth.

80-81 The heavily restored ziggurat of Ur, a step pyramid with a temple dedicated to the lunar goddess Nanna, was begun during the 3rd Dynasty of Ur (about 2050 B.C.) and reconstructed in the Neo-Babylonian period (6th century B.C.).

81 Woolley led a joint archaeology expedition by the British Museum and the University of Pennsylvania, working in Ur for 12 seasons (1922–1934). He was accompanied by his wife Katherine, whom he had married in 1927.

Agatha Christie also visited, and actually met her future husband in Ur: Max Mallowan, Woolley's assistant. There has been very little new research in Ur since the last season of excavations led by Woolley in 1934. The ziggurat was well restored and reconstructed by Iraqi archaeologists and the site, like many others, suffered damage due to the recent war in the country. Some of the objects from the excavations at Ur were preserved at the National Museum in Baghdad, but it was heavily looted in April 2003. Fortunately, the museum's most important artifacts had been secured in a bank vault. (GF)

82 top During the 1928–1929 seasons, Woolley excavated tomb PG 1237 in the royal necropolis of Ur, which he renamed the "Great Death Pit" because of the 74 sacrificed individuals buried there. He found a lyre with a bull's head at the same grave site.

82 bottom Woolley carefully handles one of the lyres found shortly after the necropolis of Ur was discovered.

83 Woolley discovered the great bull's head lyre, which is associated with funeral rituals and the sun god Shamash, in the tomb of Queen Puabi (PG 789). The front panel has lapis-lazuli and shell inlays (British Museum, London).

Leonard Woolley: The City of Ur of the Chaldeans

84-85 Found by Woolley in tomb PG 779, the Standard of Ur is a small trapezoidal box covered in mosaics of lapis lazuli and shell. The archaeologist suggested it was a royal standard, though it could also be the sound box of a musical instrument. The panel shown here is known as the "War Side" and depicts a Sumerian king in his role as military leader (British Museum, London).

86 Woolley uncovered some magnificent, highly ornate women's jewelry while digging at the royal necropolis of Ur. There were beautiful bracelets, necklaces, chokers, earrings, and headdresses made of gold, lapis lazuli, and coral. With the help of a mannequin, one begins to get an idea of the wealth represented in these individuals' grave goods (British Museum, London).

87 top The ornate women's jewelry emerges from the ground at the moment Woolley discovered it in 1929.

87 bottom The large amount of coral and lapis lazuli used in the jewelry from Ur suggests that the Sumerians developed a vast network of communication with the outside world. The lapis lazuli came from the region of present-day Afghanistan, while the coral was from the western coast of India (British Museum, London).

88-89 In 1924, Woolley unearthed a ceremonial gold helmet belonging to Meskalamdug, a Sumerian ruler buried in the necropolis of Ur, who lived around 2400 B.C. The copy is pictured here (British Museum, London).

89 Woolley found this section of an ox yoke in the tomb of Queen Puabi, at the royal necropolis of Ur. It would have been used to hitch the animals to a sled for transportation. The rings and the lower portion are silver, while the onager is made of electrum (British Museum, London).

Max Uhle:
The Father of Andean Archaeology

Affectionately known as the father of Andean archaeology, Max Uhle's pioneering exploration of sites in Bolivia, Peru, Chile, and Ecuador has had a lasting impact on the field of prehistoric South America. Born in Germany and trained as a philologist, Uhle developed a passion for archaeology during trips to the region beginning in the late 19th century, as he conducted research and gathered artifacts for museums in Dresden and Berlin. His subsequent archaeological expeditions were funded by the American Exploration Society as well as Mrs. Phoebe Hurst, the mother of publishing magnate William Randolph Hurst. Uhle went on to study and excavate numerous sites; the most famous among them are Tiwanaku and Pachacamac.

In 1892, Uhle published a volume about Bolivia's Tiwanaku, a site he had visited on one of his early trips. Sometimes called "the American Stonehenge" for its massive, standing stone blocks alien to the otherwise flat surrounding plateau, the site was occupied from about A.D. 500 to 1000, then abandoned before the Inka arrived in the 15th century.

The first detailed scientific documentation of the site, *Die Ruinenstätte von Tiahuanaco* (*The Ruins of Tiahuanaco in the Highlands of Ancient Peru*), on which he collaborated with photographer and engineer B. von Grumbkow, is still a highly regarded resource. Uhle returned to the site in 1894 eager to begin archaeological excavations, only to find that a Bolivian regiment was using the once-great city's ruins for target practice. He reported the incident to the government and asked for the site to be protected. To Uhle's dismay, the government agreed to step in and help preserve it, not only by halting excavations, but by denying Uhle permission to dig anywhere else in the country. So the intrepid adventurer crossed the border into Peru.

Uhle began conducting excavations at Pachacamac, located just south of Lima, in 1896. The important coastal religious center, which flourished under various cultures for some 1,300 years beginning around A.D. 200, drew pilgrims to its famous oracle and temples where the city's patron deity Pachacamac, god of creation and protector of crops, was worshiped.

Uhle unearthed the site's impressive architecture, including its walls and mud-brick stepped temples, or pyramids, with ramps and plazas, as well as a wide variety of ceramics, lithics, and objects made of organic materials such as feathers, shells, and bones. These finds were critical in establishing an Andean chronology, but the site is equally well known for its unusual human remains, which Uhle famously described in scientific detail.

He first wrote of uncovering a cemetery on a terrace of the temple complex that contained the remains of sacrificed *mamacuna*, or "Virgins of the Sun," a select group of women who served the temple and its priest. To the north was the Temple of Pachacamac, whose walls were decorated with colorful paintings of animals and birds; nearby were the burials of men with short-cropped hair who were likely high-ranking officials. Underneath the terrace, however, he discovered the earliest and most unusual burials, which date to around the 6th century A.D. Laid to rest inside tombs fashioned of stone and mud brick were stubby, cushiony bundles of cloth topped with heads made either of painted ceramic or wood through which unblinking inlaid shell eyes peered out.

Inside each was a human body, filled with pacae and avocado leaves, held in place by cotton shrouds and a basketlike frame. The mummies were buried with goods intended for use in the afterlife, such as gourds and ceramic vessels for food and drink.

90 Max Uhle carried out the University of Pennsylvania Museum's first South American expedition in Bolivia and Peru in 1895.

92-93 Thousands of mummy bundles—tightly flexed bodies wrapped in textiles and equipped with artificial heads—have been found at Pachacamac.

93 Uhle excavated mud-brick stepped pyramids, or temples, at Pachacamac, where the city's patron deity was worshiped. The important god needed to be appeased, as he could cause earthquakes.

92

A true scientist, Uhle noted the first "mummy bale" simply as find "no. 1044."

Recent technical studies of some mummies undertaken by the University of Pennsylvania Museum of Archaeology and Anthropology have revealed that one contained a sacrificed infant; another held a child who suffered from a mysterious health problem.

Max Uhle's careful studies, scientific field reports, and detailed publications of his remarkable discoveries remain invaluable references to scholars today. Even more important, however, his excavations captured the world's attention and brought these once-forgotten sites and cultures to light, inspiring future generations to explore the region and beyond. (EBM)

94 Tiwanaku's iconic Gateway of the Sun, an 8-ft (2.5-m) tall monolithic structure weighing more than 10 tons, depicts at its center the so-called "sun-god." Scholars suggest he may represent Viracocha, creator-god of the Inka, holding a staff and, possibly, a spear. Even today, thousands gather here yearly to watch the vernal equinox.

95 Viracocha is flanked by 30 winged beings that may represent his attendants. Scholars argue that the gateway was originally located in the site's Pumapunku temple mound, and moved to this spot around A.D. 1000. Some believe the move caused the crack; others blame the Spanish who arrived in the mid-1500s, intent on wiping out paganism.

Ernesto Schiaparelli:
The Tomb of an Egyptian Queen

Many Egyptologists explored the wadi south of the Valley of the Kings in search of tombs. In ancient times it was called the "Place of Beauties" (*Ta set neferu*); in the 19th century it was Biban el-Harim, the "Valley of the Queens." Wilkinson was there in the early 1800s, Rosellini in the 1830s, and Lepsius from 1845. But the greatest discovery there was the tomb of Nefertari, the principal queen of Ramses II. The distinction of that find went to Ernesto Schiaparelli who opened the tomb and revealed its incomparable wall paintings in 1904.

Schiaparelli (1856–1928) came from a family of scholars. He received his Egyptology degree from the University of Turin, where his father was a history professor. As director of the Egyptian Museum in Florence (1881–1883), Schiaparelli reorganized the collection. Subsequently, he founded the Italian Archaeological Mission in Egypt and was made director of the Egyptian Museum of Turin (1894–1927), which he raised to one of the world's largest Egyptian collections. Schiaparelli realized that Turin only exhibited New Kingdom artifacts, and his excavations at Heliopolis, Giza, Hermopolis, Assiut, Qau el-Kebir, Gebelein, and Aswan from 1903 to 1920 were in part designed to fill the collection's gaps. His most important publication, *The Book of Funerals of the Ancient Egyptians* (*Il Libro dei Funerali degli Antichi Egiziani*) (1882) was about Egyptian funerary text. Having stayed with Franciscan missionaries at Luxor in 1884, Schiaparelli established the Association to Succour Italian Missionaries to relieve their poverty. Nonetheless, Schiaparelli's fame rests in large part on his work in the Valley of the Queens and at nearby Deir el-Medina, where he explored the settlement and burials of the royal necropolis workers: priests, officials, craftsmen, and artists.

The Valley of the Queens was the burial place of queens and princesses, but also of princes, from the 18th to the 20th Dynasty. Eighty tombs have been identified there, 13 were found or cleared by Schiaparelli during his 1903–1905 campaign there. Nefertari's tomb had been ransacked in antiquity, but there were some pieces of the pink granite lid of her sarcophagus (the lower part had apparently been removed intact to be reused at another time) and pieces of her gilt wooden coffin. Of her mummy, there are a few fragments of the legs (now in Turin). Schiaparelli recovered potsherds, wooden servant figures (*shabtis*), and a few bits of jewelry missed or dropped by the looters.

But the glory of Nefertari's tomb was the series of inscriptions and paintings that cover its walls. In vibrant colors, the queen is shown repeatedly being presented to or making offerings to deities such as the four great goddesses, Isis, Selket, Nephthys, and Hathor. Elsewhere she appears with Osiris, lord of the underworld, and Ptah, the creator. The jackal god of embalming, Anubis, appears prominently. Texts on the walls come from The Book of Coming Forth by Day, one of the Egyptian funerary texts, intended to guide Nefertari to the afterworld and to protect her on the journey. Further protection is offered by guardians such as a winged cobra, while the goddess Ma'at, the Egyptian personification of cosmic order, extends her wings around Nefertari's cartouches, enveloping and shielding them.

The paintings, however, were more fragile than could have been imagined. The limestone in the Valley of the Queens is heavily fractured and has bands of flint running through it. So the artists applied a heavy plaster layer on the rock and into it outlined the texts and scenes. The walls were then given a gypsum wash and painted with a variety of pigments, some of which held to the surface strongly while others did not. With the opening of the tomb, the paintings deteriorated quickly and in 1934 the tomb was closed.

96 Queen Nefertari, the wife of Ramses II, was buried in a magnificently decorated tomb in the Valley of the Queens. She's wearing a vulture headdress, a symbol of female royalty, in this image from one of the tomb walls.

98-99 and 99 Records and photographs taken when the tomb was found were critical to the success of the restoration of the paintings by the Getty Conservation Institute.

A major restoration effort by the Getty Conservation Institute in 1986–1992 has saved the paintings.

Nefertari's family background is unknown, perhaps a noble line in Thebes. The inclusion in her tomb of an ivory/bone knob with the cartouche of the 18th Dynasty pharaoh Ay, who succeeded Tutankhamun, is a tantalizing suggestion of some link to him, but it would be pure speculation to say it was a familial one.

Her name means "The One to Whom Beauty Pertains." She married Ramses when she was young, bearing him at least six children before she died in her late 30s. During life, she held the titles "King's Great Wife" (the preeminent queen) and "Mistress of the Two Lands" (indicating a strong role in the affairs of Egypt, Upper and Lower). (MR)

100 top Osiris, god of the underworld, is featured on one of the walls in Nefertari's tomb. He is depicted with his characteristic green skin.

100 bottom Schiaparelli made this map of Nefertari's tomb to illustrate his published account of the discovery.

100-101 The view through the burial chamber of Nefertari toward her tomb's entrance shows priests in leopard skins depicted on columns in the foreground.

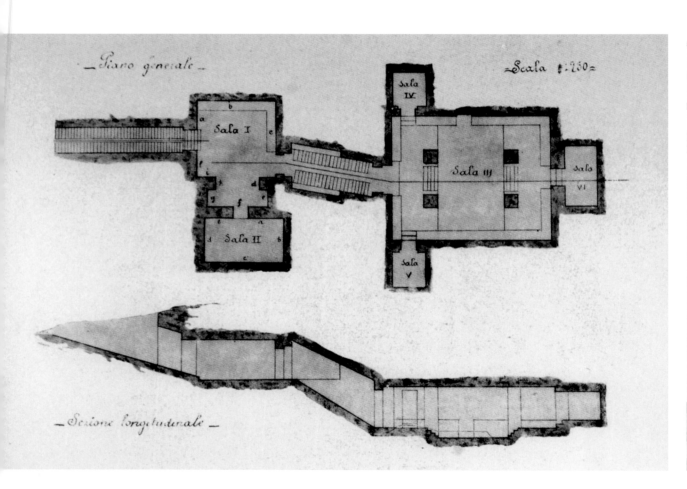

The Tomb of Kha and Meryet

102 left When Schiaparelli found the anthropomorphic sarcophagus of Kha, the architect, it was still in its original position inside the Deir el-Medina tomb (Egyptian Museum, Turin).

102 right This old photo shows the mummy of Meryet inside a wooden sarcophagus with a funeral mask covering her face. It was taken moments after she was discovered.

102-103 Egyptian workers employed by Schiaparelli for the Deir el-Medina digs, crowding around the entrances to the excavated tombs.

Two years after the discovery of Nefertari's tomb, Schiaparelli made another amazing find—the tomb of the 18th Dynasty architect Kha and his wife Meryet—during his investigations of Deir el-Medina. Arthur Weigall, who was the Egyptian Antiquities Service Inspector, described the event on a day in February: "The entrance of a passage running into the hillside was blocked by a wall of rough stones...we realized that we were about to see what probably no living man had ever seen before." The tomb was completely intact, "untouched ashes still in lamps that had burned out three thousand years earlier. One asked oneself in bewilderment whether the ashes here, seemingly not cold, had truly ceased to glow at a time when Rome and Greece were undreamt of, when Assyria did not exist, and when the Exodus of the Children of Israel was yet unaccomplished."

Buried with Kha was a royal cubit measure (21 in/52.5 cm) of made of wood covered in gilt—apparently a gift to the architect from Amenhotep II. Kha and Meryet's tomb gives us an example of what well-off middle-class Egyptians expected to use in the afterlife. Kha had his razors and scissors, Meryet her wig and cosmetic box. There was an abundance of foodstuffs, as well as clothing and linens. For entertainment, Kha had his senet board game. There were no wall paintings, but Kha was buried with one of earliest known copies of the Book of the Dead, some 46 ft (14 m) long and illustrated in color. X-rays in 1966 revealed jewelry on both mummies, which have never been unwrapped. Around Kha's neck is a heavy necklace, likely the "gold of honor" given by pharaohs to reward favored generals and officials. (MR)

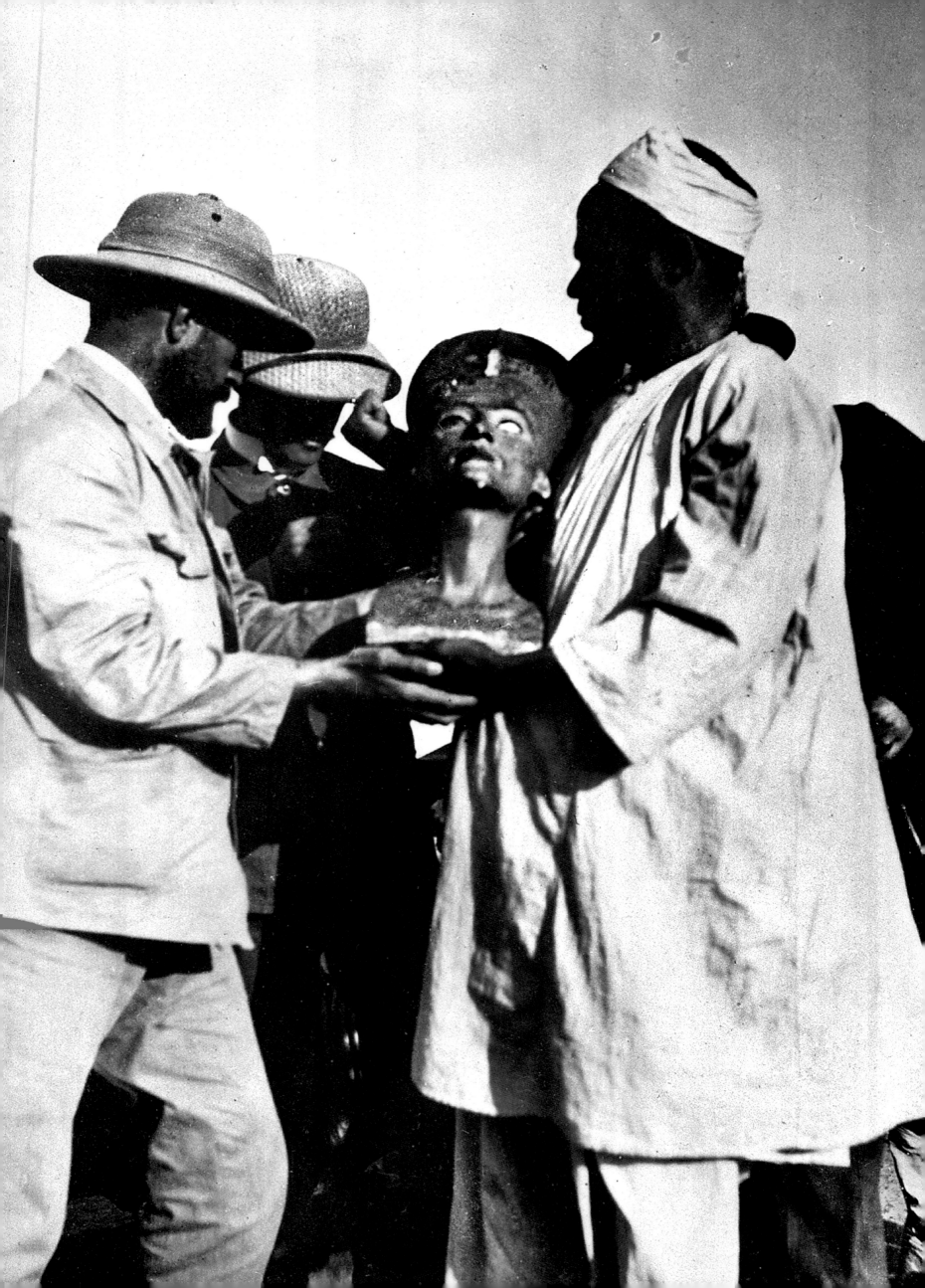

Ludwig Borchardt:
The Bust of Nefertiti

One of the best-known masterpieces of Egyptian art is the bust of the late-14th-century Queen Nefertiti. It shows her wearing a tall blue flat-topped crown (originally with a cobra rearing protectively on the front). Her long neck, high cheek-bones, gracefully arching eyebrows, and kohl-rimmed eyes, together with a faint smile, are captivating. Now in the Neues Museum, Berlin, the limestone and painted plaster sculpture was found by Ludwig Borchardt at Amarna, the capital of the "heretic" Pharaoh Akhenaten.

Nefertiti's name means, "A Beautiful Woman Has Come," but we do not know her ancestry. She was probably from an elite Egyptian family, possibly the daughter of Ay, the powerful, older courtier who succeeded Tutankhamun. It has been suggested that she might be one of the foreign princesses married to the pharaoh in political alliances, perhaps Tadukhepa of Mitanni under an Egyptian name.

Born in 1863, Borchardt studied architecture in Berlin from 1883 to 1887 before switching to Egyptology. He joined the Department of Egyptian Art at the Berlin Museum in 1895, then served with the Egyptian Antiquities Service between 1896 and 1899, helping to write the general catalogue of antiquities for the Egyptian Museum, Cairo. In 1907, Borchardt founded the German Institute for Ancient Egyptian Archaeology in Cairo, and became its first director. Retired from the Institute in 1929, he had become fascinated with the lost city of Atlantis (he thought a site in the Sahara of Tunisia might be the legendary city). In the later 1930s, Borchardt, whose family was Jewish, resided in Switzerland to escape Nazi persecution (a younger brother perished at Auschwitz) and he died in Paris in 1938.

In 1907, Borchardt began work at Amarna for the Deutsche Orient-Gesellschaft. On December 6, 1912, his crew was excavating in the southern part of Amarna in the remains of a mud-brick villa. There, in a small room, they discovered a collection of portraits. The villa had belonged to Akhenaten's sculptor Thutmose, and the pieces included more than 20 prototype plaster casts, unfinished or models with guidelines drawn on them, and carved stone heads (in quartzite of various colors), some finished except for inlays of eyebrows and eyes, others complete though missing crowns that would have been added in another material. Various identifications have been made of these: Akhenaten, Amenhotep III (his father), Nefertiti, Kiya (a secondary queen of Akhenaten's), and royal daughters.

The right eye of the Nefertiti bust retains its rock crystal inlay. What happened to the left eye is debated. Some scholars believe it was never inlaid, saying there is no glue residue in socket and suggesting the bust might have been used to show young sculptors how inlaid eyes were done. Others say that the eye was originally present but fell out at some time in the past. Intriguingly, the early photos show the bust covered with dirt, but the eye socket perfectly clean. Did the rock crystal fall out at the time of excavation? Borchardt searched for it, but to no avail.

Rumors that the Nefertiti bust might be a fake have surfaced from time to time. Doubters claim that the preservation is simply too good to be true: the only significant damage is to the front of the crown and to the queen's ears, while the face is untouched. Others argue that the esthetics of the sculpture are suspiciously close to Art Deco, the style current at the time it was found. But photographs taken at the site right after discovery show it covered with dirt. Perhaps the rumors are based on an exact copy supposedly made in Berlin and used by the museum to loan to other institutions.

Controversy surrounds ownership of the Nefertiti bust. When it was found, the practice was for excavators and Egypt

106

to divide the finds fairly. In this case, the bust went to Dr. James Simon, who funded the German dig. In 1920, Simon gave his collection to the Prussian state, and in 1924 the bust went on public display. The Egyptian press immediately demanded its return, claiming that the division of finds had been rigged, with Borchardt leaving the bust uncleaned so that its value would go unnoticed. Diplomatic pressure increased for the return in the mid-1930s when the Nazi regime wanted to foster ties to Egypt, but Hitler, a devotee of the bust, decided against it.

An Egyptian approach to the German government in 1978 met with no success. More recently, Zahi Hawass, head of Egypt's Supreme Council for Antiquities, has asked that the Nefertiti bust be returned, the issue being highlighted in 2003 when the Berlin Museum curators allowed the bust to be briefly placed on a full-size bronze body and filmed together as artwork. This called into question the museum's claim that the bust is too fragile to travel for even a short-term loan to Cairo. (MR)

104 Professor Hermann Ranke, an Egyptologist from the Deutsche Orient-Gesellschaft, observes the bust of Nefertiti on December 6, 1912. It had just been found among the ruins at Amarna.

107 Since it was found, the bust of Nefertiti has fascinated scholars and antiquity enthusiasts with its remarkable and timeless beauty. Nearly 100 years have passed since the discovery, and the debate over its ownership still has not died down (Neues Museum, Berlin).

108 left Ludwig Borchardt found various works in plaster among the ruins of Thutmose's sculpture workshop, including this one, which bears the features of Queen Nefertiti (Neues Museum, Berlin).

108 right Borchardt found this plaster bust, possibly a depiction of the young Tutankhamun, while excavating at Amarna (Neues Museum, Berlin).

109 Borchardt searched long and hard, but ultimately in vain, for the rock crystal inlay that would complete the left eye of the Nefertiti busts (Neues Museum, Berlin).

"Yes, wonderful things":
Howard Carter and the Tomb of King Tut

November 26, 1922. Valley of the Kings, Egypt. Three men and a woman face a door that was walled up and sealed in antiquity. They hold their breath as one of the men punches a hole in the millennia-old plaster. He nervously raises a candle in the open space and observes what is beyond the door. The tense silence of anticipation is broken by one of the people behind him. "Can you see anything?" "Yes, wonderful things." Howard Carter had just opened the tomb of Tutankhamun. From that moment archaeology would never be the same.

Carter was born in England in 1874. He was only 17 years old when he arrived in Egypt to work as an artist on archaeological missions conducted under the Egyptian Exploration Fund. His job was to reproduce the images and inscriptions found in pharaonic monuments. Collaborating with such high-caliber archaeologists as Percy Newberry, Edouard Naville, and William Flinders Petrie, he quickly learned the techniques and secrets of Egyptology. He acquired solid field experience and training by participating in the excavations at Amarna, in the Deir el-Bahri temple of Hatshepsut, and some Middle Egypt sites. In 1899, at just 25 years old, Carter was appointed Chief Inspector of Antiquities in Upper Egypt by the Egyptian Antiquities Service. It was a prestigious position that made him responsible for research conducted on archaeological sites around ancient Thebes. One of his first projects was organizing the transportation to Cairo of royal mummies that were found in 1898 by Victor Loret, a French Egyptologist, at the tomb of Amenhotep II in the Valley of the Kings, a location that would become an obsession of Carter's for the rest of his life.

Meanwhile, in 1900, Carter had uncovered the cenotaph of the pharaoh Montuhotep II at the end of a tunnel dug in the Deir el-Bahri plain. But Carter's greatest wish was to take up his own excavations in the valley, where he hoped to make discoveries like Loret's. He did some digging between 1902 and 1904, taking ad-

vantage of financing from Theodore Davis, a wealthy American lawyer who owned a concession in the valley. He managed to identify the tombs of Hatshepsut and Thutmose IV. But in 1904, he was transferred to Lower Egypt as the new Chief Inspector of the region. In 1905, there was a brawl between the Egyptian guards at Saqqara and some inebriated French tourists. Carter backed up his guards in the dispute. It escalated into a diplomatic incident and Carter being disciplined. Carter remained in Egypt and earned a living by selling his drawings of ancient monuments. In 1907, he met a wealthy English nobleman, Edward M. Herbert, the Earl of Carnarvon. Herbert was in Egypt to take advantage of the hot, dry climate, which was ideal for treating his respiratory problems, and had obtained a concession for digging in the Valley of the Kings. The two began a working partnership that lasted until World War I broke out, though their searches yielded no exciting results. When the war ended, Carter and Carnarvon returned to work in the Valley of the Kings, where they'd again obtained a concession for digging.

Carter's dream was to find the tomb of Tutankhamun, a little known 18th Dynasty pharaoh who lived at the end of the Amarna period. The pharaoh's name was carved on some of the objects buried in the valley. The archaeologist began systematic and meticulous excavations in search of the entrance to a tomb, inspecting the areas that had not yet been explored. But despite his efforts the results he hoped for did not come. In the summer of 1922, Carnarvon decided that the next season would be Carter's last chance and then he would stop financing the project. Carter began digging again on November 1 of that year, concentrating on a triangle of earth facing the entrance to the tomb of Ramses VI. The remains of some huts belonging to workmen who had excavated the tomb itself were already immersed in the sand. The place seemed promising, but it hadn't been explored be-

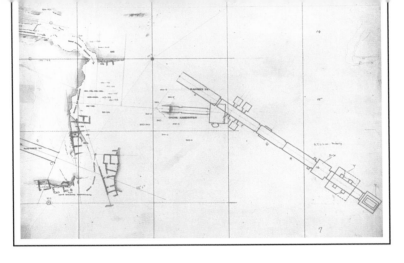

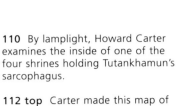

110 By lamplight, Howard Carter examines the inside of one of the four shrines holding Tutankhamun's sarcophagus.

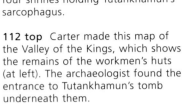

112 top Carter made this map of the Valley of the Kings, which shows the remains of the workmen's huts (at left). The archaeologist found the entrance to Tutankhamun's tomb underneath them.

112 bottom The Valley of the Kings is an unusual location for a party, but refreshments were served to the archaeology team members to celebrate the discovery of Tutankhamun's tomb.

113 The entrance to Tutankhamun's tomb, protected by a stone wall, was discovered in front of the entrance to the tomb of Ramses VI (center).

cause it was too close to the path that led tourists around the Valley of the Kings everyday. Carter's team found a step dug into the rock on November 4, right under one of the huts. In the following days there were 16 more steps uncovered, leading to a closed door that was walled in and sealed. There was no doubt that Carter had found a new tomb in the valley.

On November 6, he telegraphed Carnarvon in England: "At last have made wonderful discovery in valley; a magnificent tomb with seals intact; re-covered same for your arrival; congratulations." On November 23, Lord Carnarvon and his daughter, Evelyn, joined Carter in the Valley of the Kings. American engineer Arthur Callender had already arrived to assist in the operation. The walled-up door had been opened and resealed in antiquity, and the seals and cartouche of Tutankhamun were legible on it. Beyond the door, Carter found a descending corridor full of rubble, which was cleared by No-

vember 26. That day, Carter opened a hole in the sealed door at the end of the corridor and looked upon the wondrous treasures of Tutankhamun's tomb for the first time. Though it had been broken into by tomb raiders in the pharaonic age, it had not been completely looted like all the other tombs in the valley. In fact, the pharaoh's store of grave goods had remained nearly intact. News of the amazing discovery spread quickly and the Valley of the Kings was flooded with journalists, curious onlookers, and authorities, coming to watch the process of clearing out the artifacts, which Carter had begun with extremely meticulous care. It took Carter's team eight years to clear the tomb of the nearly 3,500 objects inside. During this time, the finds were catalogued, photographed, restored, and finally shipped to the Cairo Museum, where they are on display today.

The first section of the tomb, the antechamber, was full of randomly piled objects: chariots, funerary beds, wooden chests and

114 top The walled-up door in the antechamber, which leads to the burial chamber, is flanked by two wooden statues of the pharaoh. Once the plaster was removed, Carter saw the first gilded wooden shrine.

114 bottom Carter, his assistant Arthur Callender, and an Egyptian helper prepare the wooden statues found in the antechamber for transport.

115 The wooden statues from the antechamber, painted black and covered in gold laminate, both depict Tutankhamun (Egyptian Museum, Cairo).

containers, weapons, alabaster jars, chairs and stools, jewels, and clothing. But the most valuable item was surely the king's golden throne, with a magnificent depiction of the young pharaoh and his wife, Ankhesenamun, on the back. The objects stacked in a small area (annex) off the antechamber were removed between 1927 and 1928. In the antechamber, two wooden statues of Tutankhamun acted as sentinels for another walled up door. This door was officially opened on February 17, 1923, revealing the contents of the burial chamber. The only section of the tomb with painted walls, the burial chamber was almost completely taken up by large shrines of gilded wood, which clearly contained the pharaoh's sarcophagus. The burial chamber led to the last room, the treasure chamber, where more incredible objects were piled. Among them was a statue of the god Anubis, in the form of a jackal, on a sedan chair. A gilded wooden tabernacle held four alabaster containers (canopic jars) with the mummified organs of the pharaoh. One of the most delicate, difficult, and emotional periods of the discovery, the burial chamber kept Carter and his team busy from 1924 to 1925. Carnarvon couldn't help in this crucial phase of the work, as he died in April 1923, immediately fueling the myth of the "pharaoh's curse."

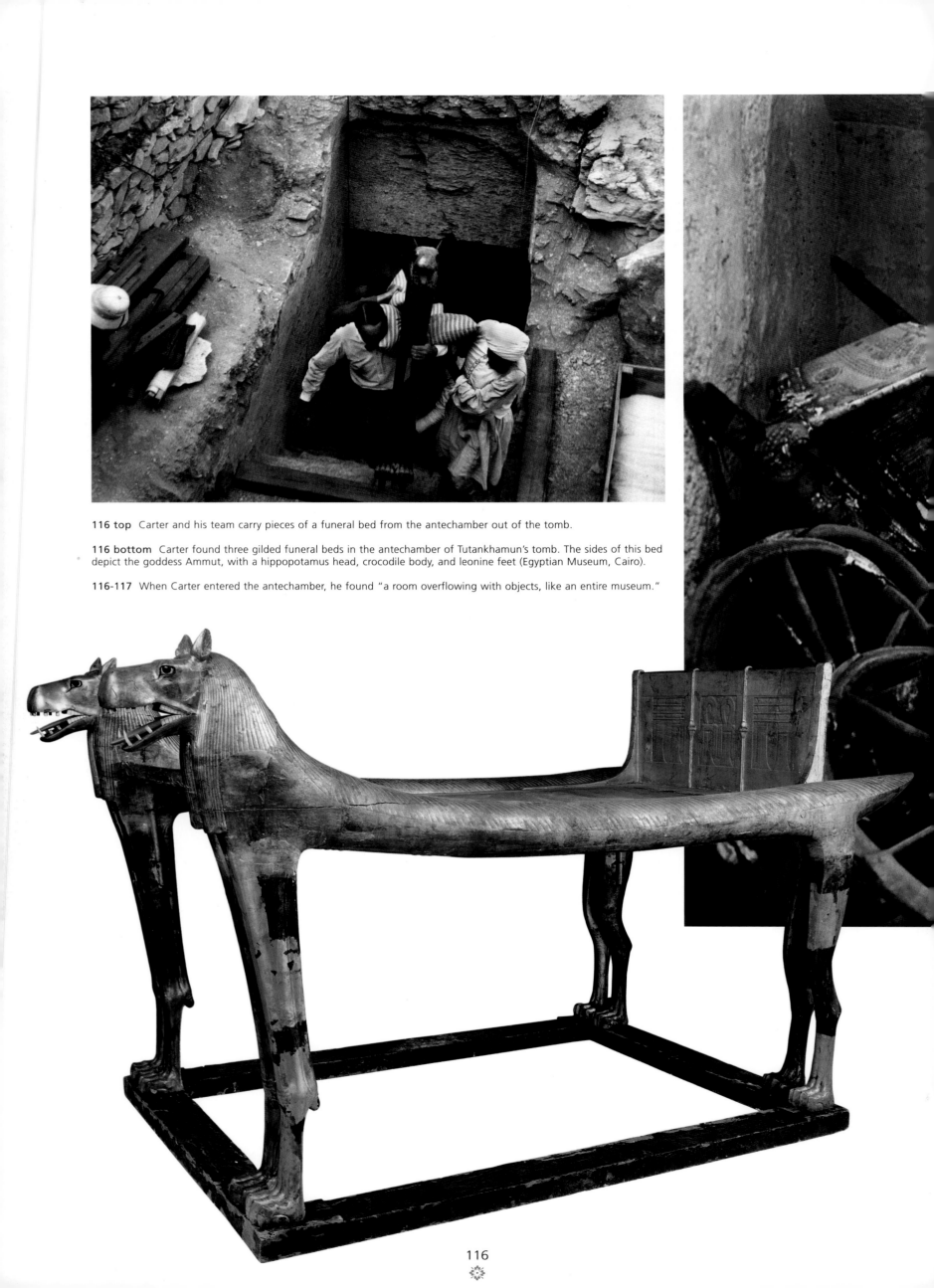

116 top Carter and his team carry pieces of a funeral bed from the antechamber out of the tomb.

116 bottom Carter found three gilded funeral beds in the antechamber of Tutankhamun's tomb. The sides of this bed depict the goddess Ammut, with a hippopotamus head, crocodile body, and leonine feet (Egyptian Museum, Cairo).

116-117 When Carter entered the antechamber, he found "a room overflowing with objects, like an entire museum."

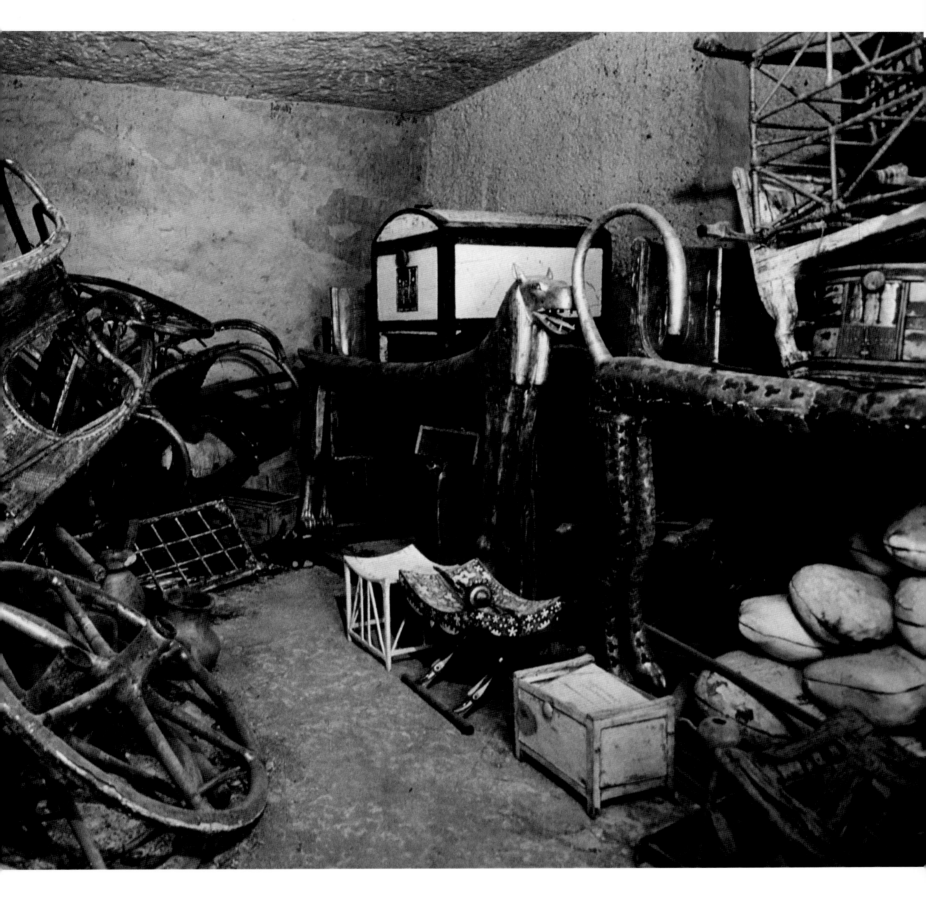

The large gilded wooden shrine contained another three just like it, which had to be carefully dismantled and removed to reach the pharaoh's quartzite sarcophagus. Working by lamplight in narrow spaces, Carter's team removed the stone cover on February 12, 1924, and found themselves looking at the first of three anthropomorphic sarcophagi that protected the mummy of Tutankhamun. The first two were wooden and covered in gold laminate, while the innermost was made of solid gold, one of the most valuable ancient items ever found.

On October 28, 1925, the solid gold cover of the inner sarcophagus was removed and Carter gazed Tutankhamun. The face of the pharaoh who had died at a very young age, was covered in a magnificent gold funerary mask, the most famous piece of pharaonic art ever found.

118 The canopic jars with Tutankhamun's remains were placed in this gilded wooden shrine with four statues of protective goddesses on the sides (Egyptian Museum, Cairo).

119 top In the tomb's Treasure Chamber, Carter found this gilded wooden chest sitting on a sedan chair. A statue of the god Anubis in the form of a jackal had been placed on top (Egyptian Museum, Cairo).

119 bottom The jackal was found wrapped in a piece of linen, which bore the date of Tutankhamun's birth.

On November 11 Carter began to examine the mummy, which was not in a good state of preservation. Numerous amulets and precious jewelry were taken from the bandages. Tutankhamun's mortal remains were thus returned to history and to the interest of scholars; the life of this ancient ruler is still researched and questioned today, so many years after the discovery. The discoverer himself died in London, in 1939, with the honor of having made what is perhaps the greatest archaeological find of all time. (GF)

120 Carter found this wooden sculpture of Tutankhamun in the antechamber. He believed it was used as a mannequin (Egyptian Museum, Cairo).

120-121 It took Carter's team 8 years to remove all the items from the tomb.

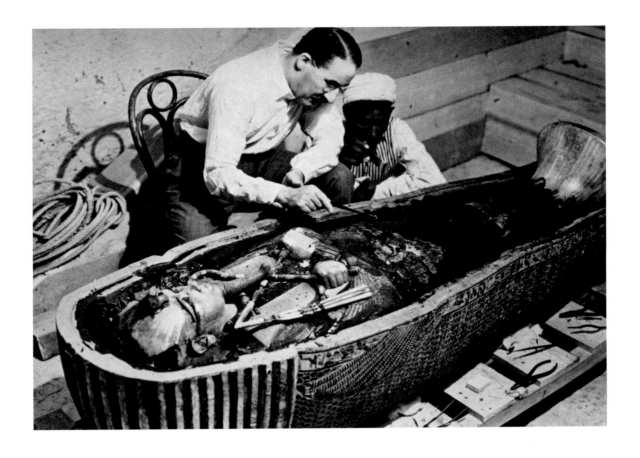

122 It took Carter a long time to remove the splendid gold funerary mask from Tutankhamun's face because the unguents used in the mummification process acted like a glue (Egyptian Museum, Cairo).

123 top Carter very carefully cleans the gluelike resin from the third sarcophagus holding the body of the dead pharaoh. In October 1925, the archaeologist finally managed to view the mummy of Tutankhamun.

123 bottom After removing the stone sarcophagus and the first anthropomorphic sarcophagus, Carter found a wooden sarcophagus covered in gold laminate and inlays. The facial features suggest that it may not have been originally intended for Tutankhamun (Egyptian Museum, Cairo).

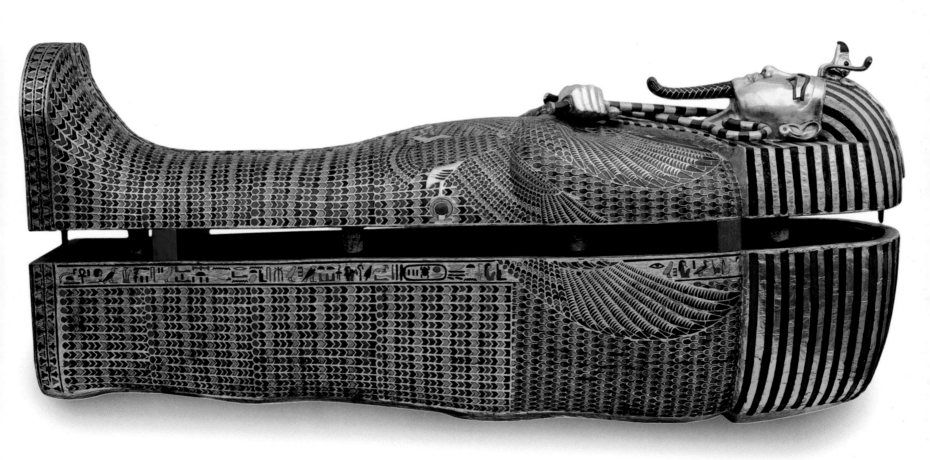

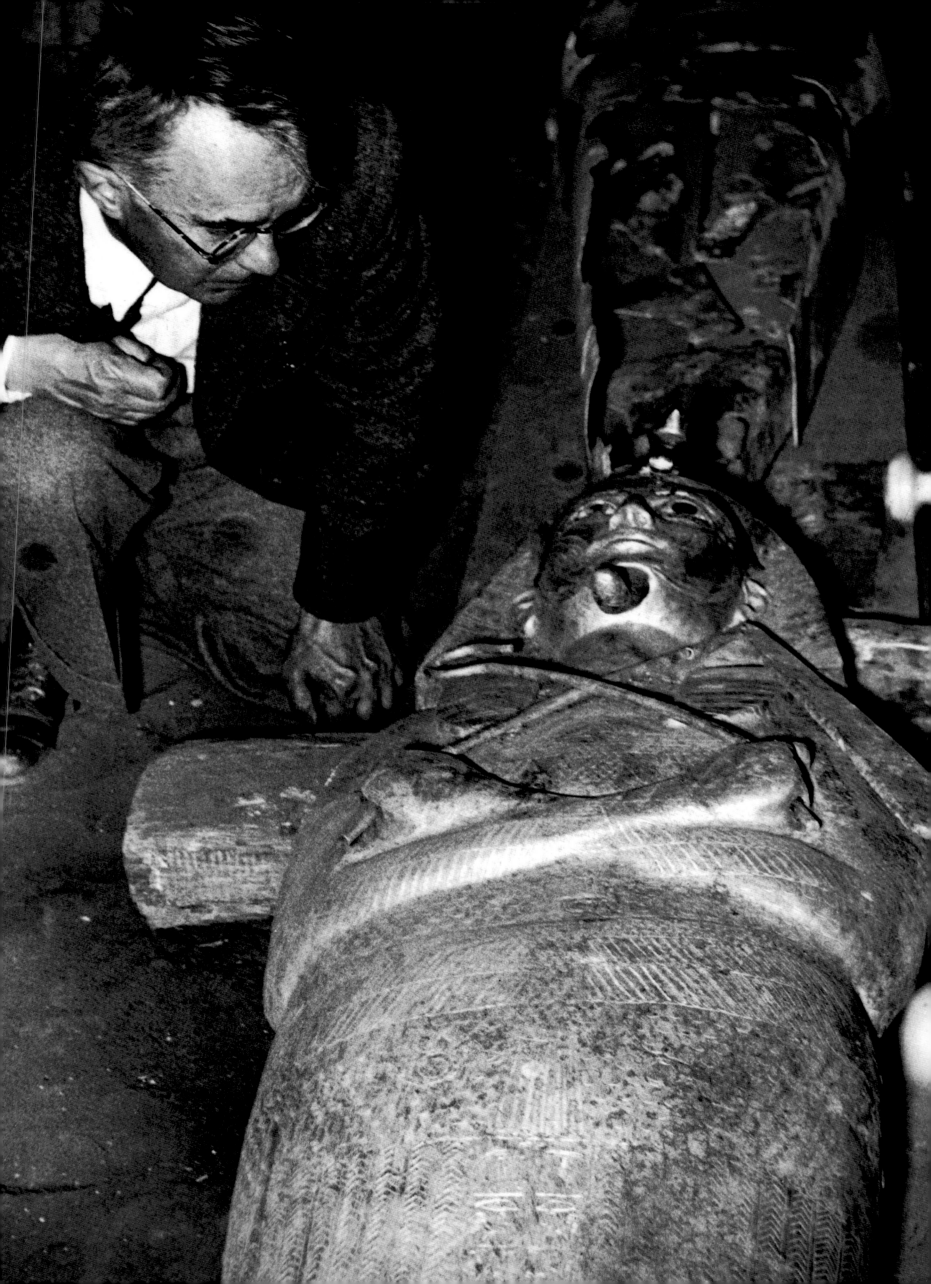

Pierre Montet:
The Royal Necropolis of Tanis

After Howard Carter's incredible discovery of Tutankhamun's tomb and the treasures within, many Egyptologists harbored the hope that they, too, would find the tombs of kings and recover their valuable grave goods. This fortunate fate was bestowed upon French Egyptologist Pierre Montet, who unearthed royal tombs belonging to rulers from the 21st and 22nd dynasties at the Egyptian site of Tanis.

Born in 1885, Montet began his work in the field doing on-site research for the Institut Français d'Archéologie Orientale in Cairo (IFAO) at Abu Rawash, Assiut, and Beni Hasan. He dug at the Lebanese site of Byblos throughout the 1920s, discovering the city's royal burials. He taught Egyptology at the University of Strasbourg between 1919 and 1948, then at the Collège de France from 1948 to 1956. He directed archaeological digs at Tanis between 1929 and 1940, around present-day San el-Hagar in the northwestern Delta. When World War II broke out, he was forced to put the excavations on hold until he could resume between 1946 and 1956. His archaeological digs were instrumental in reconstructing the history of the settlement, which became the capital of the Pharaonic Kingdom in the 9th century B.C., during the Third Intermediate Period. Archaeologists such as Auguste Mariette and Flinders Petrie had already visited the site in the 19th century. They had identified ruins as the Hyksos capital of Avaris and moved some of the monuments found on-site to major European museum collections, but the systematic excavations really started under Montet's direction. Based on all the monuments found from the Ramesid era, he identified the site as Pi-Ramses, Ramses II's capital, which is mentioned in the Bible (Book of Exodus). The monuments had actually been seized from preexisting sites by rulers of the 21st Dynasty and their successors, then transported to Tanis for the purpose of founding a new Delta capital, a sort of "northern Thebes."

Various sacred sites were identified at Tanis. The main site was a large temple complex dedicated to the god Amun, who inspired the corresponding southern god Karnak. Founded by Psusenes I, it was expanded during the 30th Dynasty and in the Ptolemaic Period. Two other temples were associated with the main sanctuary, dedicated to the gods Mut and Khonsu, who were an integral part of the foremost divine trinity in Egyptian worship.

On February 27, 1939, Montet made the greatest discovery of his life: the royal necropolis of the 21st and 22nd Dynasty rulers, located within the sacred walls of Amun's temple. The first grave he found belonged to Osorkon II (22nd Dynasty). Although it had been robbed in antiquity it provided some valuable artifacts, like the quartzite sarcophagus of Takelot I. On March 20 of the same year, Montet uncovered a second tomb in the royal necropolis, this time untouched, which turned out to be the tomb of Psusenes I (21st Dynasty). In his own words, the archaeologist found "marvels worthy of *A Thousand and One Nights*" inside the tomb. Among them was a silver sarcophagus with falconlike features belonging to Sheshonq II, whose mummy had a splendid golden funerary mask. The sarcophagus was opened in the presence of Egypt's King Faruk, who came to the site specifically to attend the event. While Montet continued his research in the royal necropolis of Tanis, the events leading up to World War II were taking place in Europe, a tragedy that would inevitably obscure any news of the exceptional finds made by the French archaeologist. Before he was forced to abandon the site because of the war, Montet managed to enter the tomb's burial chamber on February 15, 1940. Inside he found the grave of Psusenes I himself: the king's remains were preserved in a red granite sarcophagus (taken from 19th Dynasty Pharaoh Merenptah), which contained another anthropoid sarcophagus made of granite, and yet another made of silver.

When he opened the last sarcophagus and found himself face to face with the pharaoh's magnificent gold funerary mask, now on display with the rest of the treasure in the Cairo Museum, Montet must have felt the same emotions as his colleague Carter. He found the grave goods of another pharaoh, Amenemope (21st Dynasty), in the chamber originally reserved for Psusenes I's mother, Queen Mutnodjmet.

The treasure of Tanis, one of the greatest ancient Egyptian finds of all time, included pectorals, vases, and other jewelry made of gold and precious stones. In 1946, after the war ended, Montet was able to resume his research at the tomb of Psusenes I, where he found rich grave goods in another chamber that belonged to a general called Wendjebauendjed.

When Montet died in 1966, excavations continued at the site and the project became known as "Mission Française des Fouilles de Tanis." It was directed by Jean Yoyotte for 20 years, then by Philippe Brissaud from 1985 to the present. His recent research has been concentrated around the sacred site dedicated to Amun and inside the sacred walls of the temple of Mut. Field studies continue to provide further details about the structure and organization of the buildings in ancient Tanis, helping to increase understanding of how it was conceived and modeled after the southern city of Thebes, and eventually became the quintessential religious center of Lower Egypt. (GF)

124 Pierre Montet examines the silver sarcophagus of Psusenes I, which contained the pharaoh's remains.

126 The archaeology mission directed by Montet uncovered a large statue of the goddess Sekhmet next to the pharaoh Ramses II, in the ruins of the temple of Mut at Tanis.

127 In this photo, taken during Montet's excavations at Tanis in the 1930s, the stone blocks that once made up the monumental gateway to the temple of Amun are scattered on the ground.

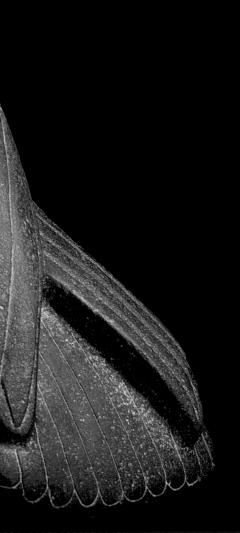

128 and 129 top One of Montet's great discoveries at Tanis was a statue of
Ramses II. The statue spells out the pharaoh's name in symbols: the falcon
god Horus as *Ra*, the child *mes*, and the sedge stalk *su* held by the child,
or Ramesses, which we shorten to Ramses.
(Egyptian Museum, Cairo).

129 bottom The falcon's beak was missing when the statue of young
Ramses II was found, but it turned up in a different area of the site.

130 Montet examines the inside of the anthropomorphic red granite sarcophagus of Psusenes I, just after it was opened.

130-131 and 131 center This red granite sarcophagus was originally made for the 19th Dynasty Pharaoh Merenptah, but it was reused by Psusenes I. Montet found it in his tomb at Tanis (Egyptian Museum, Cairo).

131 top The covers of the four canopic jars of Psusenes I depict the four children of Horus. Montet found them next to the pharaoh's red granite sarcophagus (Egyptian Museum, Cairo).

132 In 1940, Montet poses next to the outer anthropomorphic sarcophagus of Psusenes I, which was removed from his tomb. The tomb itself had been found a year earlier inside the sacred enclosure of Amun's temple at Tanis.

133 The outer anthropomorphic sarcophagus containing Psusenes I had also been usurped from a previous owner, probably an official from the 19th Dynasty (Egyptian Museum, Cairo).

134 Montet found the tomb of Psusenes I and the splendid gold funerary mask covering his face on February 15, 1940. News of the discovery, second only to Tutankhamun in terms of value, was obscured by the tragic wartime events that were devastating Europe at the time (Egyptian Museum, Cairo).

135 Made of silver, the internal anthropomorphic sarcophagus of Psusenes I is one of the magnificent treasures that emerged from Montet's excavations at Tanis (Egyptian Museum, Cairo).

Alberto Ruz Lhuillier:
Face to Face with King Pakal

Eternally enshrouded in a layer of fine mist more than 3,000 meters above sea level overlooking the Gulf of Mexico, the Late Classic Maya city of Palenque thrived during the 7th century A.D. Some 1,300 years later, archaeologist Alberto Ruz Lhuillier—a pre-Columbian specialist who was born in Paris, France; educated in his father's native Havana, Cuba; and later became a Mexican citizen—began to unravel its secrets. Although the Spanish first came across the site in the mid-16th century, it was Ruz's 1952 discovery of the tomb of K'inich Janaab Pakal, or "Pakal the Great," who ruled the city between A.D. 615 and 683, that ignited intense interest in both the ancient Maya and the site of Palenque, where intriguing finds are being made to this day.

While Palenque, nestled in a dense forest of cedar, mahogany, and sapodilla trees, was founded hundreds of years earlier, the city-state only began to flourish when Pakal, a *kuhul ajaw* or "divine lord," ascended the throne. Its population, power, and level of artistic sophistication soared as he began massive construction projects, including a four-story "palace" where ceremonies were held. The monumental stone building was covered with stucco carvings of rulers and gods, and featured interior courtyards and a stream with running water—a great engineering feat that ensured Palenque's success. During this time, however, Palenque had many economic and political rivals, including the city-states of Calakmul and Toniná, with whom it competed for control of land, raw materials, and trade routes. It is believed that Pakal began his aggressive building campaign because so many structures had suffered damage from attacks. Palenque ultimately fell around A.D. 800, not long after the death of Pakal.

Pakal the Great, as Ruz was to discover, was laid to rest in a hidden chamber of the so-called "Temple of Inscriptions," an eight-stepped pyramid where Maya hieroglyphs, including one of the longest known to date—featuring 617 glyphs—were discovered. Often carved onto architectural stone surfaces, the Maya written language, both phonetic and ideographic, assigned a meaning to each picture, which could be formed into words, sentences, and even stories. While it is believed that most people could read at least some hieroglyphs, only priests and high-ranking members of society, including the *kuhul ajaw*, could read inscriptions in their entirety.

Ruz began investigating the Temple of Inscriptions in 1949, hoping to find out how it was built. Instead, beneath a small amount of rubble, he came across a stone slab and two steps that appeared to continue down inside the structure. It took his team three excavation seasons to clear an additional 400 tons of rubble; workmen tirelessly brought it to the surface bucket by bucket, only taking breaks when small finds such as pottery and human bones—perhaps sacrificial victims—were discovered.

In June 1952, Ruz famously shined his flashlight into a dark chamber some twenty-two meters from where the team had started burrowing. He thus illuminated a narrow, vaulted room with limestone walls, containing a richly decorated sarcophagus—with a five-ton stone lid that had to be raised later with car jacks—holding Pakal's skeletal remains. It must have been a marvelous sight: sculptures, stucco reliefs and glyphs depicting the ruler becoming a divine being after his earthly existence, as well as scenes from Maya mythology. As Ruz later recalled:

"Out of the dim shadows emerged a vision from a fairy tale, a fantastic, ethereal sight from another world. It seemed a huge magic grotto carved out of ice, the walls sparkling and glistening like snow crystals. Delicate festoons of stalactites hung like tassels of a curtain, and the stalagmites on the floor looked like drippings from a great candle. The impression, in fact, was that of an abandoned chapel. Across the walls marched stucco figures in low relief. Then my eyes sought the floor. This was almost entirely filled with a great carved stone slab, in perfect condition."

But it is Pakal's exquisite burial mask made of jade—expertly crafted to reveal his supple, high cheekbones, prominent nose, and curvy

136 This rare jade funerary mask was covering Pakal's face when his remains were discovered. It depicts the *kuhul ajaw*, or ruler, of Palenque who ascended the throne at age 12 after attacks had damaged the city. The arts flourished under him, as he undertook a massive rebuilding campaign from A.D. 615 to 683 that defined his great legacy (National Museum of Anthropology, Mexico City).

138 This stucco mask found in Palenque may be a portrait of the great ruler (National Museum of Anthropology, Mexico City).

139 Discovered in a vaulted chamber, Pakal's elaborately decorated limestone sarcophagus lid depicts the king at the moment of his death, descending into the Maya underworld so he could be reborn as an ancestral deity.

lips—that perhaps most captivated the world's attention. A true masterpiece of ancient art, his wide-open eyes, made of shell, mother of pearl, and obsidian inlay are frozen in an unearthly gaze; his ears ornamented with square jade plugs and projecting rods; his chest draped with nearly a dozen strands of beaded necklaces. Each detail provides a snapshot of the care and attention the Maya elite lavished on their appearance.

Yet the full story of the site is still unraveling. Recent excavations conducted under the auspices of the Palenque Project—a joint venture of the Pre-Columbian Art Research Institute (PARI) and Mexico's National Institute of Anthropology and History (INAH)—have continued to yield extraordinary finds, including a 12-ft-tall limestone tablet depicting K'inich Ahkal Mo' Nahb' III, another ruler of Palenque, and his subjects, as well as a possible throne emblazoned with more than 200 inscribed glyphs, unearthed in a nearby temple mound, and a tomb decorated with the first painted murals ever found at the site. (EBM)

140 and 141 Alberto Ruz Lhuillier examines a stucco head he unearthed of Pakal. Its hairstyle resembles the silky strands surrounding an ear of corn, thus evoking the Maya maize-god. The famous archaeologist insisted on being buried at the site, and his tomb lies near its entrance, just before the Temple of Inscriptions (National Museum of Anthropology, Mexico City).

142-143 Pakal's tomb was found deep inside the Temple of Inscriptions, which was specially designed to house it. Each of the temple's 69 stairs represents a year of the king's reign.

Manolis Andronikos:
The Tombs of the Macedonians

In November 1977, Greek archaeologist Manolis Andronikos began excavating a great earthen mound, or tumulus—some 43 ft (13 m) high and 360 ft (110 m) across—in Vergina, the ancient Macedonian capital of Aigai, near Thessaloniki in northern Greece. As he dug into its belly, Andronikos came across fragments of grave stelai. Even deeper, he began to unearth lavish tombs that date to the 4th century B.C., filled with incredible items made of gold, silver, bronze, and ivory. Later excavations were to reveal a total of ten royal burials, most of which had been plundered.

The entrance to the only undisturbed tomb, which is 31-by-18 ft (9.5-by-5.5 m), resembles a Doric temple, and was sealed with a marble door. Above it, there was a painting depicting a hunting scene. Inside was a marble sarcophagus that contained a golden larnax, or funerary casket, holding the ashes and bones of a cremated male individual who was between 35 and 55 years old, along with his crown. The lid of the larnax bears the so-called "Vergina Sun," the starburst that is iconographically associated with the ancient royal family of Macedon. The burial chamber also housed his weapons and armor.

Based on these spectacular discoveries, Andronikos believed that he had found the final resting place of King Philip II of Macedon, a successful military leader who lived from 382 B.C. until his assassination at age 46 in 336 B.C. at his daughter's wedding. Philip II displayed his military prowess as he conquered much of Greece and quieted political unrest in Macedonia. He thus paved the way for his son, Alexander the Great, to begin his massive military campaign that stretched over a vast territory, from Greece to the Middle East to India. Two small ivory portrait heads in the tomb were interpreted as images of the famous father and son.

In the relatively smaller antechamber of the tomb were the cremated remains of a female individual, also ensconced in a similar yet smaller golden larnax, with a royal diadem. This burial, Andronikos believed, belonged to Cleopatra, the seventh or eighth wife of Philip II, who was killed immediately after her husband.

Today, however, many scholars dispute these interpretations. Recent research shows the finds from the tomb may actually date to 317 B.C., nearly two decades after the king's death. Also, although a wound was found in the cremated male individual's right eye, scholars argue that such a fierce warrior sustained even more injuries, which are not present on the remains. It has therefore been suggested that the cremated male is Philip III Arrhidaeus, one of Alexander's less-well-known half brothers.

Although he ascended the throne after Alexander's death, Arrhidaeus was more a limp figurehead than a capable ruler. The 2nd-century A.D. Greek historian Plutarch writes that the mother of Alexander, Olympias, realizing the weak mental capabilities of Philip Arrhidaeus, tried to poison him at a young age to eliminate a potential rival of Alexander for the throne. Additional forensic information—including the fact that the bones of the individual showed little physical stress—obtained in the 1990s supports this theory. The process of cremation, however, seems to have destroyed the critical evidence necessary to confirm it, so the identity of the man buried here remains a mystery.

"For many years to come, the interpretation of these finds is sure to provoke discussion among scholars," Andronikos later wrote in *Treasures of Ancient Macedonia*, an exhibition catalogue produced by the Archaeological Museum of Thessaloniki where the finds are on view. "The excavator who had the good fortune to make this discovery is the first to admit that he has uttered the first but by no means the last word on the subject." (EBM)

144 Manolis Andronikos, a professor at the Aristotle University of Thessaloniki, received the Grand Cross of the Order of the Phoenix, Greece's highest honor, for his remarkable discovery of royal tombs at Vergina.

146 top The Tomb of Philip II, which contained fantastic items such as the deceased's armor, had not been touched by looters. Fragments of five grave stelai, including one that depicts a warrior, were found in the great mound that covered it.

146 bottom The tomb's façade, decorated with triglyphs and metopes, resembles a Doric temple. Measuring 31 by 18 ft (9.5 by 5.5 m), its impressive entrance features a marble door.

146-147 This quiver made of gilded silver is lined inside with leather and adorned outside with embossed scenes that depict a military campaign culminating in the ransacking of a town (Archaeological Museum, Thessaloniki).

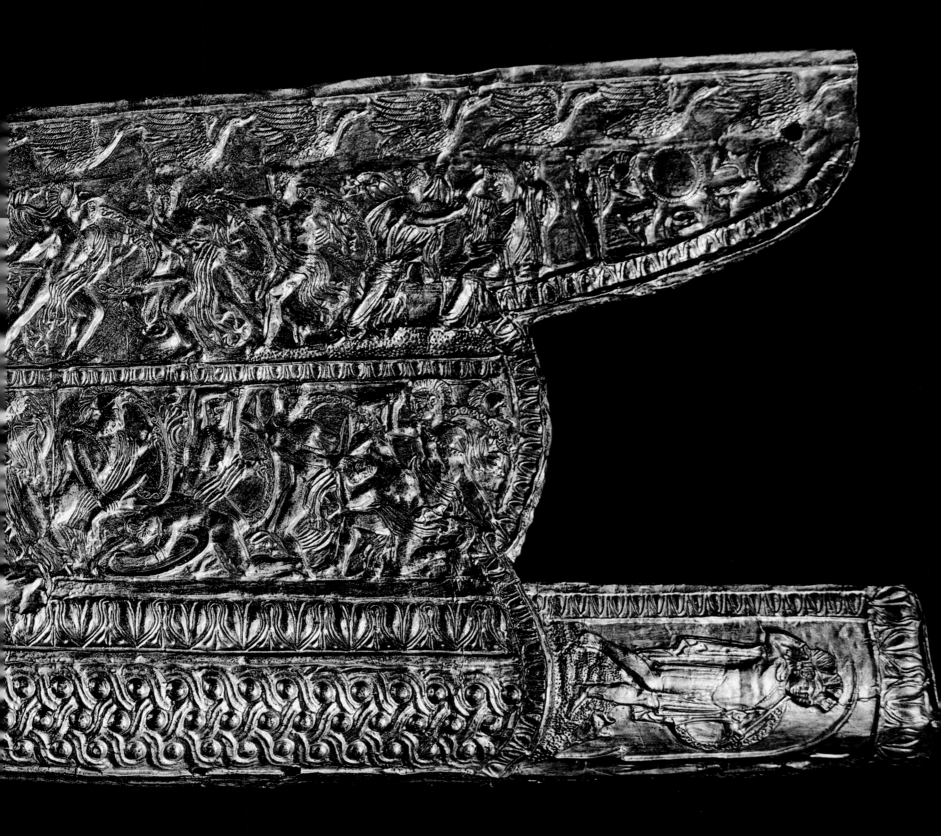

148 top Discovered inside the great larnax (below), this gold wreath was meant to honor the wealthy man buried there. Wreaths were also used during one's lifetime in religious ceremonies. This impressive example weighs 25 oz (714 gr) and is decorated with 68 acorns and 313 oak leaves, the latter of which were sacred to the god Zeus (Archaeological Museum, Thessaloniki).

148 bottom This 1.25-in (3-cm) high gold appliqué, one of several originally affixed to a garment, depicts the head of the *gorgon* Medusa, a female creature with hair made of snakes whose stare alone could turn men to stone (Archaeological Museum, Thessaloniki).

148-149 The cremated remains of a male individual, possibly Philip II, were placed in this gold larnax, or funerary chest, along with the magnificent gold wreath also shown on this page. The larnax, which has four lion feet, is decorated with a 16-pointed starburst, the emblem of the Macedonian royal family, and adorned with rosettes and floral designs (Archaeological Museum, Thessaloniki).

150 This resplendent cuirass, or breastplate, is made of iron and trimmed with gold decorations, including the heads of lions (Archaeological Museum, Thessaloniki).

151 This miniature head carved of ivory measures only 1.25 in (3 cm) tall. Some believe the bearded figure may be a portrait of Philip II (Archaeological Museum, Thessaloniki).

Viktor Sarianidi:
The Hidden Treasures of Afghanistan

Sometimes archaeological research can become so inextricably linked to the events of modern history that it dictates the fate of a discovery. Such is the case for the Tillya Tepe treasure, whose history is tightly bound to the tragic events in modern Afghanistan. Soviet archaeologist Viktor Sarianidi, a Bronze Age expert, was trying to increase understanding of the urban civilization in Bactria-Margiana when he began his excavations in 1969. He was working around the Shibergan oasis in northern Afghanistan, near the course of the Amu Darya River (Oxus River in ancient sources), a few miles from the Uzbekistan border. At the end of the excavation season, the Soviet-Afghani team directed by Sarianidi was working on a hill known as Tillya Tepe ("golden hill").

On November 13, 1978, the archaeologists' shovels hit a grave containing a rich supply of gold. With the end of the season looming, the archaeologists rushed to explore the area. They found six contemporaneous graves on the side of the hill and recovered a total of more than 20,000 magnificently crafted gold objects. The position of a seventh grave was also identified, but it was covered back up to be excavated in the following season. Sarianidi's discovery yielded exceptional results. The Tillya Tepe tombs unveiled a dark chapter in Central Asian history (1st century B.C.–1st century A.D.), when the Hellenistic Greco-Bactrian Kingdom, heir to the conquests of Alexander the Great, was overwhelmed by the migration of nomadic populations. Among them, the Yuezhi of China, who would originate the Kushan Empire (1st–3rd centuries A.D.) in the following centuries.

The six tombs uncovered at Tillya Tepe belonged to elite members from one of these nomadic tribes, who established themselves in northern Afghanistan at the threshold of the Christian era. These six, simple, rectangular graves contained several more wooden coffins wrapped in fabric. Five of them were high-ranking females, and only one was a warrior. In addition to the warrior's weapons (bows, sword, dagger, sheath), the tombs contained a rich collection of jewels and ornaments, including: crowns, pendants, earrings, brooches, necklaces, bracelets, anklets, and rings. These items demonstrate the high standards of goldsmithing found in the nomadic populations. From a stylistic point of view, the finds indicate various influences, and their eclectic composition reflects contact with the different cultural areas of the region: China, India, and the Hellenistic world. In the treasures of Tillya Tepe, a representation of the goddess Athena rests alongside the animal themes that are typical of the steppe, and the figure of a Greek soldier is next to that of a Chinese carriage pulled by dragons. Three of the women were buried with mirrors produced in China, while one of them wore a Shiite head covering. The necropolis was dated to the 1st century A.D., based on Parthian coins found in the graves, along with a Roman coin from the reign of Tiberius.

After all the objects were inventoried, Sarianidi closed the site, hoping to return to work there the next year. But the Soviet Army invaded Afghanistan in 1979 and a war began, which would be long and painful for the country and make further excavations impossible. The items from the Tillya Tepe treasure were packed in crates and transported to the National Museum in Kabul for safekeeping. Sarianidi wouldn't see them again for 25 years. The years of war with the Soviets were followed by the even more tragic years of civil war among *mujaheddin*, which lasted until the Taliban came to power. Over this period of time, all traces of the Tillya Tepe treasure vanished so completely that the international community believed it might have been lost forever to thieves, raids, or bombings. The treasure resurfaced in 2003, after the Taliban regime fell, following military intervention led by the Americans due to the events after 9/11.

It was in the Central Bank of Afghanistan vault, where it had been secretly transferred and watched over by the staff of the National Museum in Kabul.

In the presence of Sarianidi himself, the crates were reopened and the contents examined, determining that the treasure had remained virtually intact. The historical memory and contemporary world heritage of a country so tragically torn apart by war was thus salvaged by the courageous initiative of a few Kabul Museum staff members.

Since 2006, the contents of the Tillya Tepe treasure have been shown outside the borders of Afghanistan for the first time, in a traveling exhibit that has visited several European and U.S. cities. (GF)

152 Viktor Sarianidi found this pendant of gold and precious stones among the grave goods of a female buried in Tomb II at Tillya Tepe. Together with a companion piece, it formed the ornament for the deceased's headdress (National Museum, Kabul).

154 and 155 The 1978 Soviet-Afghani archaeological mission directed by Sarianidi led to the discovery of six tombs and their rich stores of artifacts, which amounted to more than 20,000 pieces.

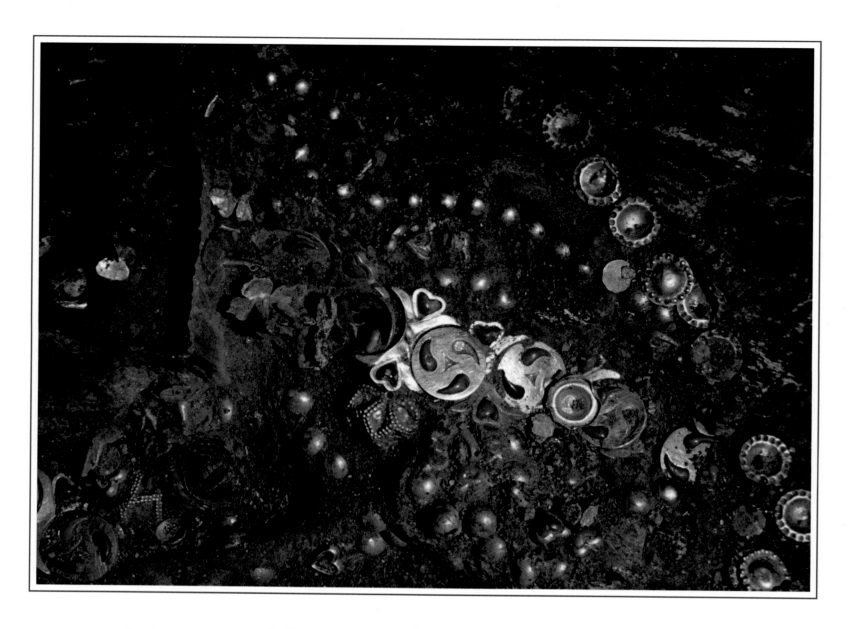

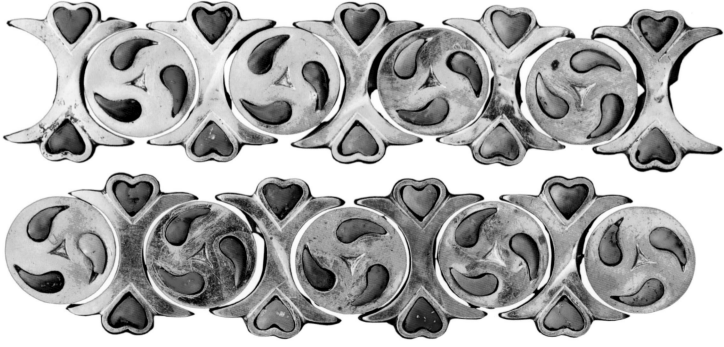

156 and 157 bottom Sarianidi found these gold and turquoise beads in Tomb II at Tillya Tepe. They formed
a necklace arranged in vertical bands under the neckline of the clothing on the deceased.
The tomb was one of three female burials discovered at the site (National Museum, Kabul).

157 top The individual buried in Tomb IV at Tillya Tepe wore richly ornamented shoes with two buckles like the ones
shown here. Made of gold and turquoise, the center depicts a man driving a chariot pulled by two winged felines
(National Museum, Kabul).

158-159 Sarianidi found this gold and turquoise clasp in Tomb VI at Tillya Tepe, along with another similar clasp; the two are symmetrical. The clasp held together the clothing of the young woman buried in the grave. It depicts a Dionysian scene: Dionysus and Ariadne ride a monstrous creature, while the hairy Silenus receives a cup of wine from them and a winged Nike holds a wreath over their heads (National Museum, Kabul).

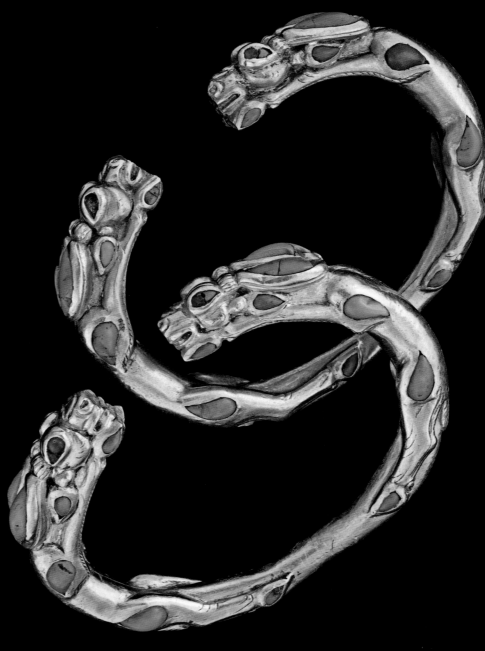

160-161 The young woman buried in Tomb VI at Tillya Tepe wore this rich and complex gold crown, surmounted by elements that form trees that are completely covered in rosettes (National Museum, Kabul).

161 These bracelets were part of the grave goods belonging to a female found in Tomb II at Tillya Tepe. They are made of gold, turquoise, and coral, with antelope heads at each end (National Museum, Kabul).

Walter Alva:
The Lords of Sipán

One night in February 1987, the director of the Brüning Museum of Lambayeque in northern Peru was woken up by a phone call from the local police. They invited him to come take a look at some archaeological finds that had just been taken by grave robbers. Walter Alva could not have known that the phone call would change his life, leading to some of the biggest archaeological discoveries in the Andes. The grave robbers had started looting the ruins of two mud-brick pyramids known as the Huaca Rajada, near the village of Sipán in the Lambayeque Valley. A splendid golden head with lapis-lazuli inlays particularly attracted Alva's attention. He immediately recognized it as an object belonging to the elite class of the Moche culture, which developed along the dry coastal area of northern Peru between the 1st and 7th century A.D.

The Moche culture was mainly based on agriculture, which was made possible by the complex irrigation systems they built. It's best known for its refined pottery, which is highly admired and bears artistic depictions that provide a window into the religious beliefs, mythology, divinities, and social organization of this ancient Andean civilization. The Moche built large brick pyramidal monuments as tombs for high-ranking individuals. They were highly skilled in metalworking as well, forging splendid jewelry and symbols of power. Having recognized the importance of the find, Alva decided to proceed with archaeological excavations on the site immediately. He was also motivated by a desire to prevent more illegal plundering, which had begun as soon as news of the discovery spread. A team of archaeologists formed, and once the difficulties stemming from lack of funds and the presence of grave robbers had been overcome, excavations began in the Huaca Rajada area, around an adobe platform near the pyramids.

After four months of work, Alva's team discovered the burial chamber of a Moche ruler, the first one of its kind to be found intact. The high-ranking individual, who was named the "Lord of Sipán," had died between the ages of 45 and 55. The mummy was buried in a wooden sarcophagus, and the wealth of grave goods included ornaments and jewelry made of gold, silver, and gilded copper, with lapis-lazuli and shell inlays. Among them was a crown associated with lunar worship and a scepter-knife. Another eight people (servants, concubines, and warriors) had been buried next to the body, along with some animals (llamas and dogs). Niches in the burial chamber walls contained hundreds of ceramic vases with molds of prisoners and warriors, which were used to hold food offerings.

When they had finished exploring the burial chamber of the "Lord of Sipán" and recovered all the fragile objects, Alva's team proceeded to the mud-brick platform. There they uncovered a second burial chamber belonging to a priest, which was contemporaneous with the previous one and just as intact. This find also included objects and ornaments of valuable workmanship. When the archaeologists moved on to the lower level of the structure, which corresponded to the oldest phase in the building's history, they found a third tomb belonging to another high-ranking individual, probably a ruler from an earlier period. The "Old Lord of Sipán" mummy had also been buried in a wooden coffin and was surrounded by a wealth of grave goods, including a funerary mask and various necklaces and pectorals, not to mention some gilded copper platelets that depicted the divinities of the Moche pantheon. In this case, the body was buried with a young woman and a llama.

The discoveries made by Alva provided invaluable information about the social organization, hierarchical evolution, religion, and power system of the Moche culture, in addition to providing the first direct glimpse into the funeral practices and beliefs of this population and its elite members.

The excavations at the archaeological site of the Huaca Rajada are still going on today, and other tombs belonging to various people of lower ranks have been uncovered over the years, providing further information about Moche society. The Royal Tombs of Sipán Museum was inaugurated in 2002, with Alva as director. The museum's goal is to evaluate the results of the discoveries, promoting culture and historical research related to the Peruvian region. In 2007, Alva found a cave painting while digging at the Ventarrón temple, not far from Sipán. It dates to about 2000 B.C., and might represent the oldest archaeological evidence of that nature in the Americas. (GF)

162 Walter Alva examines a copper Moche scepter that was found during the first excavations around the Lord of Sipán's tomb. The Peruvian archaeologist conducted research at the three Moche pyramids of Huaca Rajada for 20 years. It culminated in 2002, when the Royal Tombs of Sipán Museum opened with Alva as director.

164-165 This gold ear ornament was the first object that Alva and his team saw when they opened the coffin containing the Lord of Sipán's remains. In the center is a Moche warrior with a scepter and a shield, wearing a crescent-shaped headpiece and a nose piece (*nariguera*). He is flanked by two other warriors made of turquoise (Royal Tombs of Sipán Museum, Lambayeque).

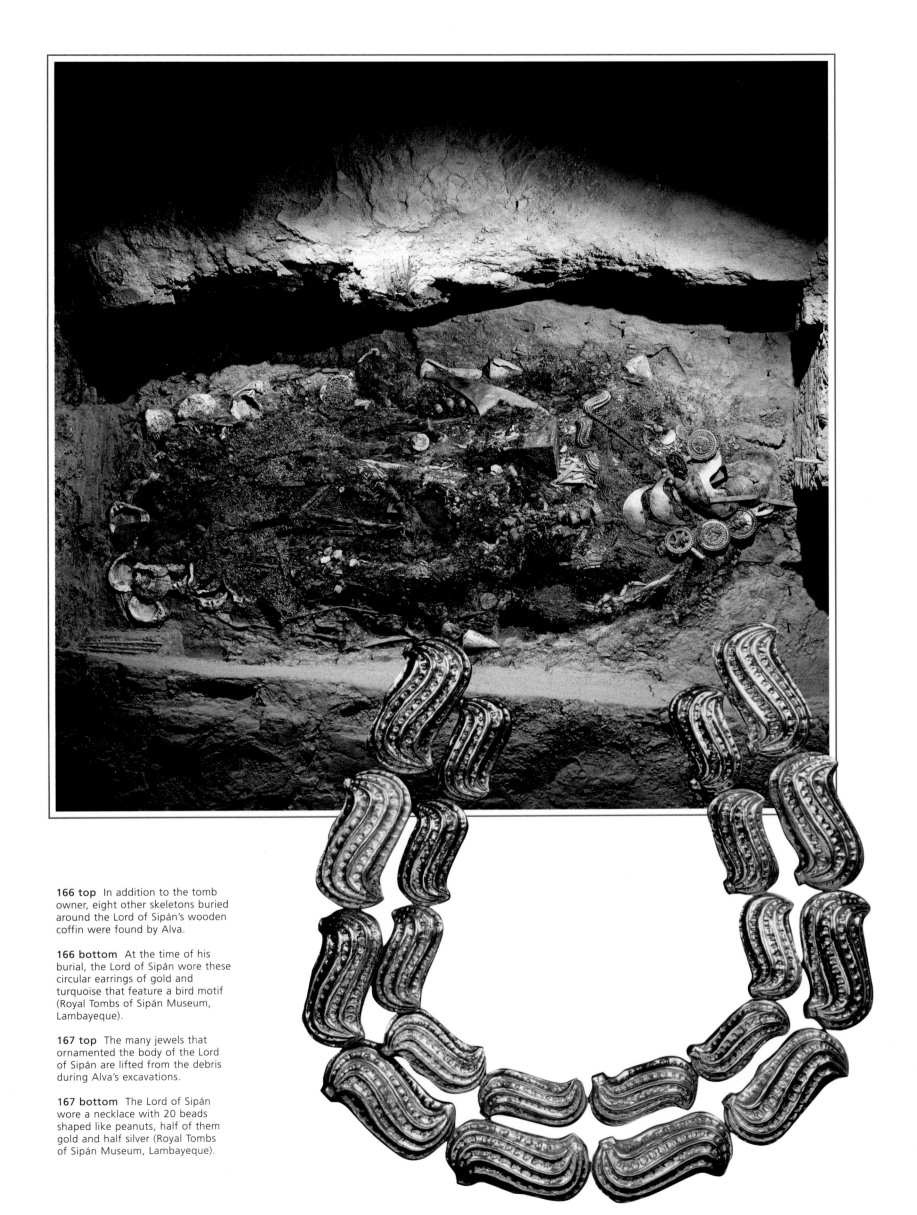

166 top In addition to the tomb owner, eight other skeletons buried around the Lord of Sipán's wooden coffin were found by Alva.

166 bottom At the time of his burial, the Lord of Sipán wore these circular earrings of gold and turquoise that feature a bird motif (Royal Tombs of Sipán Museum, Lambayeque).

167 top The many jewels that ornamented the body of the Lord of Sipán are lifted from the debris during Alva's excavations.

167 bottom The Lord of Sipán wore a necklace with 20 beads shaped like peanuts, half of them gold and half silver (Royal Tombs of Sipán Museum, Lambayeque).

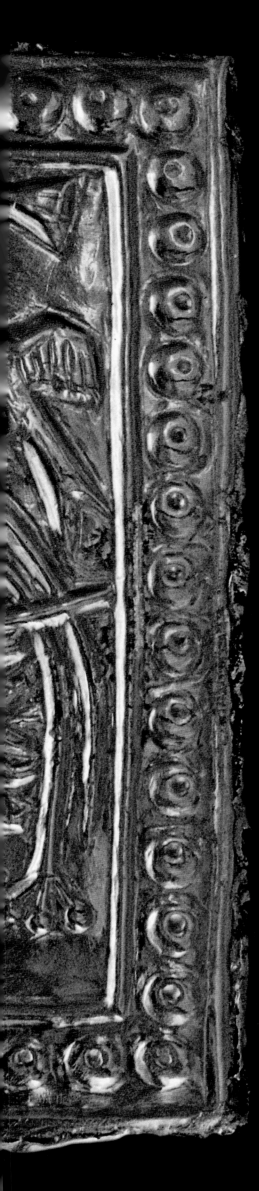

168-169 The greatest symbol of power found in the Lord of Sipán's tomb is a gold and silver scepter-knife. The upper portion of the gold handle (shaped like an upside down pyramid) depicts a war scene in relief: a Moche warrior holds a prisoner by his hair (Royal Tombs of Sipán Museum, Lambayeque).

169 Walter Alva found this copper ornament on the Old Lord of Sipán's body. It depicts a feline with anthropomorphic features, probably an ancient Moche deity. The teeth are made of shells and there are two serpents on the forehead (Royal Tombs of Sipán Museum, Lambayeque).

170 Paolo Matthiae's team found the royal archive of Ebla in 1975. It contained more than 17,000 clay tablets, making it a highly valuable source for studies of the ancient Near East. (National Museum, Aleppo)

172-173 This sacrificial basin decorated in relief was found at Temple N in Ebla, which is dedicated to the sun god Shamash. (National Museum, Aleppo)

Paolo Matthiae:
Ebla and Its Clay Empire

The name "Ebla," an ancient city in the Syrian Desert, was known by scholars because it appeared in various cuneiform inscriptions from Mesopotamia and was cited in the annals of Thutmose III at Karnak, but its ruins had never been found. In the 1950s, the fortuitous discovery of a basalt basin decorated with relief carvings near Tell Mardikh, a small hill about 34 miles (55 km) south of Aleppo, provided the evidence to start searching for the city. In 1964, the Tell Mardikh excavations were entrusted to the Sapienza University of Rome under the direction of Italian archaeologist Paolo Matthiae, a project that is still active today.

The main structures from the inhabited areas were uncovered during the first archaeological digs. The city occupied about 150 acres (60 hectares) and the most important public buildings, palaces, and temples were found on a central high ground, or acropolis. The lower city, with stores and private residences, extended in a circle over the underlying flatland. There were four entry gates in the high fortified walls, which defended the inhabited center. In 1968, an Akkadian inscription was found on a basalt statue depicting King Ibbit-Lim, which confirmed that the archaeologists were indeed excavating the ruins of ancient Ebla. But the site of Ebla would not catch the attention of the international press until an exceptional find by Matthiae's team in 1975: thousands of inscribed clay tablets, which made up the city's royal archives, were found among the ruins of palaces on the acropolis. The tablets were still stacked as they had been the moment the archive was abandoned, though they were once lined up on wooden shelves or collected in ceramic containers. They provided extensive and invaluable information on the city and the ancient Near East, with which Ebla had a close relationship. Written in cuneiform script, the tablets were in Eblaite, a Semitic language unknown

until that point, which was deciphered by Giovanni Pettinato from the University of Rome. Their content was mostly economic and administrative in nature, and revealed that Ebla was at the center of a tight network of trade with the surrounding area around the middle of the 3rd millennium B.C.

Raw materials from Anatolia, the Iranian plateau, India, Egypt, and the Red Sea passed through the city. Other than trading, the population's main livelihoods were agriculture, sheep farming, and craftsmanship (textiles and metalworking). There was one ruler at the head of the city, with a staff to assist in public administration. During the period of its greatest expansion (proto-Syrian era) around 2350 B.C., Ebla came to control a vast portion of Syrian land, managing several vassal cities and building a network of diplomatic relations with bordering states. Conquered by Sargon of Akkad around 2300 B.C., the city entered a new phase of development at the beginning of the 2nd millennium B.C. (paleo-Syrian era). It then began to decline, until it was definitively destroyed by the Hittite army around 1600 B.C.

In more than 40 years of archaeological excavations, the Italian team has uncovered many valuable items in addition to the tablets. These include fine examples of royal statuary, gold jewelry from the tombs of princes, ivory carved in the Egyptian style, and altars and basins, not to mention Egyptian objects dating to the Old Kingdom and the Second Intermediate Period. The discovery of Ebla helped trace the history of urban civilizations and how they developed outside the traditional territories of great river civilizations (Egypt and Mesopotamia) throughout the course of the 3rd millennium B.C. It also allowed for the study and comprehension of dynamics and relationships among the political entities of the ancient Near East during the Bronze Age. (GF)

Jean-Yves Empereur:
Sunken Alexandria Treasures

The city of Alexandria, Egypt, was one of the most important metropolises in the ancient world—a leading cultural center and major commercial hub on the Mediterranean during the Greco-Roman era and a point of contact between Asia and the Far East, Africa and the Mediterranean. Alexander the Great founded the city in 331 B.C. As the capital of the Ptolemaic Egypt, Alexandria was renowned for its cultural institutions (the museum and the library) and the famous lighthouse, or Pharos, located just off the coast on the like-named island of Pharos. The lighthouse was built by Ptolemy II and was considered one of the Seven Wonders of the World. Today, Alexandria is a modern city, and the architectonic layers built up over centuries have buried the vestiges of the ancient city and its monuments. But the sea has preserved some of the city's ancient treasures. Alexandria was subjected to a series of cataclysmic natural events (earthquakes and tsunamis) beginning in the 4th century A.D. The sections of the city that were right on the water sank below sea level, taking their monuments with them. The idea that the sea had preserved remnants of Alexandria and its monuments had circulated at least since the Napoleonic era, but the hypothesis had never been fully tested beyond some superficial research in the 1960s.

In 1994, the Egyptian authorities commissioned an underwater archaeological salvage mission from the Center for Alexandrian Studies, to be directed by French Egyptologist Jean-Yves Empereur. Empereur's team expected to find the remains of the lighthouse in the waters off the Mameluke fortress of Qaitbay, where cement blocks were about to be placed to form a breakwater. The underwater archaeologists on Empereur's team began diving, cataloguing and studying a large number of ancient, carved, stone blocks scattered on the seafloor. They were helped by modern instruments such as GPS and computer graphics, used to reconstruct the position and structure of the buildings.

The archaeologists found fragments of columns and statues, various sphinxes, and a few obelisks, some of colossal proportions. These objects were pulled from the water in 1995 and are now on exhibit at an open-air museum near the Roman Theater. Among the recovered objects were an obelisk from the Pharaoh Seti I (19th Dynasty) and a splendid calcite sphinx that belonged to Psamtik II (26th Dynasty). A colossal statue of one of the first Ptolemaic rulers (possibly Ptolemy II) was recovered from the sea in two pieces and placed in front of the new Library of Alexandria building. According to Empereur's team, some architectural elements of the lighthouse structure were identified among the many stone blocks on the seafloor, some weighing up to 70 tons (64 metric tons).

The Center for Alexandrian Studies isn't the only institution that has been concerned with underwater exploration along the coast of Alexandria in recent years. Frank Goddio—a former financial consultant from France who has dedicated himself full time to underwater archaeology—and his underwater research society started exploring some areas of the port in 1996. He identified the now submerged island of Antirhodos, where the ancient port structures stood. It was home to the city's royal quarter and the site of Cleopatra's palace. Thanks to the work of underwater archaeologists, many items were pulled from the waters: statue fragments, obelisks, sphinxes, and writings from the pharaonic, Ptolemaic, and Roman eras that have shed new light on the city's history and helped trace a detailed map of the Portus Magnus before it sank. Goddio's underwater exploration also extended to the bay of Aboukir, where his team managed to locate the remains of the French fleet sunk by Nelson in the "Battle of the Nile", as well as the ruins of cities that were deep below sea level for centuries (Canopus, Heraklion, and Menouthis) and recover some of their sunken treasures. (GF)

174 This granite head from the colossus of Ptolemy II was lying at the bottom of the Alexandria harbor.

176-177 A diver from Jean-Yves Empereur's team moves toward a sphinx bearing the cartouche of Ramses II.

178-179 and 179 Divers prepare the cables that will be used to remove this colossal statue of Ptolemy II, which might once have decorated the famous lighthouse, from the harbor of Alexandria.

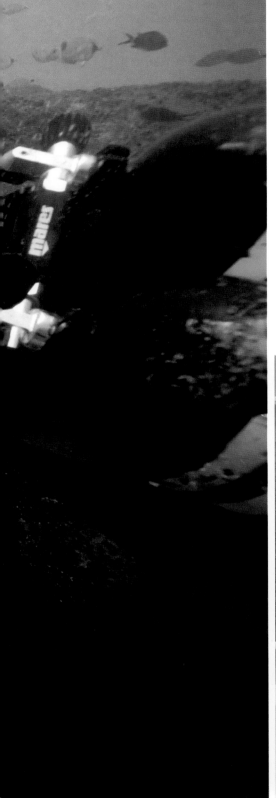

Zahi Hawass:
The Valley of the Golden Mummies

"I need the sand and the dust the way others need water and food. Archaeology is my life, my love, my passion," says Zahi Hawass, head of Egypt's Supreme Council of Antiquities. The man who has single-handedly brought archaeology in Egypt into the 21st century, Hawass is familiar to many people from his television appearances, but he is also a serious scholar, an authority on the Giza Plateau and author of books including *Silent Images: Women in Pharaonic Egypt*, *The Lost Tombs of Thebes*, and *The Valley of the Golden Mummies*.

One of Hawass's first media coups, the "Valley of the Golden Mummies," was discovered in 1996 in the Bahariyah Oasis some 240 miles (380 km) west of the Giza pyramids. Consisting of a number of collective tombs, which Hawass believes may hold up to 10,000 mummies, the cemetery site dates from the late 4th century B.C. through the 4th century A.D. At the time of the discovery, however, the Bahariyah antiquities department did not have enough funding or trained excavators or conservators, so further investigation was put off until 1999.

Delay for such reasons, while necessary, is symptomatic of what Hawass has spent the past two decades changing. The future, he says, includes implementing site management policies, limiting new excavations by foreign institutions to areas most in need of work, building more museums throughout the country, improving the training of guards and archaeologists, educating the public about the importance of its ancient heritage, and tracking down stolen Egyptian antiquities worldwide.

"I have a wonderful talent. I can speak to the people and bring ancient Egypt into their homes and their hearts. By showing people the magic and mystery of Egypt, tourism has increased, and this is vital to the economy of Egypt." That's another way of saying Hawass can tell a good tale. And the tale of the discovery of the Valley of the Golden Mummies is a good

one: the donkey of a site guard at Bahariyah wandered off one day, crossing the sands for over half a mile (about one kilometer), then suddenly stopping. A colleague of the guard went and fetched the donkey, but the animal refused to go home with its owner. It would only go back to that same spot—an entry to a tomb.

Cut into sandstone, the subterranean tombs at Bahariyah have an entrance room or vestibule and one or more rooms behind with niches or platforms on which the mummies were placed. The subsequent investigation and work beginning in 1999 revealed some 253 well-preserved mummies of men, women, and children. Many of them had elaborate face masks and chest plates of painted and gilded *cartonnage* (similar to papier-mâché). The spectacular "golden" mummies are of upper-class individuals from the prosperous Greco-Roman period of Bahariyah when it was a major wine-producing area. The cemetery might have begun around 323 B.C., after a temple to Alexander was built nearby.

Combining classical and Egyptian traditions, the mummies have portraitlike face masks but arre decorated with traditional motifs: the Hall of Judgment (where the deceased's soul was assessed); Ma'at, goddess of Truth; Anubis, god of embalming and the necropolis; and the four Sons of Horus, who guarded the dead. Among the artifacts found in the tombs were figurines of mourning woman with their hands upraised, earrings and bracelets, food trays and wine jars, coins, and glass vessels that would have held kohl (eyeliner) or ointments for the deceased to use in the afterlife.

Later seasons at Bahariyah focused on conservation and site management. The mummies left in place were treated to protect them from deterioration and infestation. Ceilings, doors, and ventilation were installed to protect and maintain the tombs.

180 Zahi Hawass works in Tomb 54, one of the largest tombs discovered during the 1999 excavations, in the Valley of the Golden Mummies.

182-183 Egyptian archaeologists work in Tomb 54 at Bahariyah, which has two funeral chambers with niches dug into the walls to hold the mummies.

183 Hawass carefully removes sand from the gold funerary mask of a female mummy found in Tomb 54.

Today, a museum is being built at the site to accommodate the increasing numbers of tourists.

Bahariyah is just one of the many high-profile projects that Hawass has used to bring ancient Egypt to the world. Now he is involved with analyzing the DNA of the royal mummies and investigating a mysterious passage in the tomb of Pharaoh Seti I in the Valley of the Kings. In 1968, Hawass joined the Department of Antiquities but did not like the job. After trying to switch to a dioplomatic career, he returned to archaeology. Assigned to an excavation in the Delta, he recalls, "One day, I found a tomb with a beautiful statue. I took a brush and started to clean the sand from the statue—at that moment, I found that the eyes of the statue were looking at my eyes and this touched my heart. I had found my love, and my love is archaeology!" (MR)

184 The mummies found at Bahariyah were from the Greco-Roman era. They were neatly aligned in the niches, and their bandages were wrapped in geometric patterns.

184-185 The mummies of individuals from the lower classes were wrapped in simple bandages, but those from more prominent families bore masks and necklaces of gilded *cartonnage*.

186-187 One of the most ornate and well-preserved mummies found in Tomb 54 is known as "Mummy C." The head, neck, and shoulders were covered in *cartonnage* painted with various funerary deities. A flower garland made of stucco rests atop the black curls that frame the young woman's gilded face. This high-ranking individual from the Greco-Roman era also bears a royal uraeus on her forehead (Museum of Bahariyah).

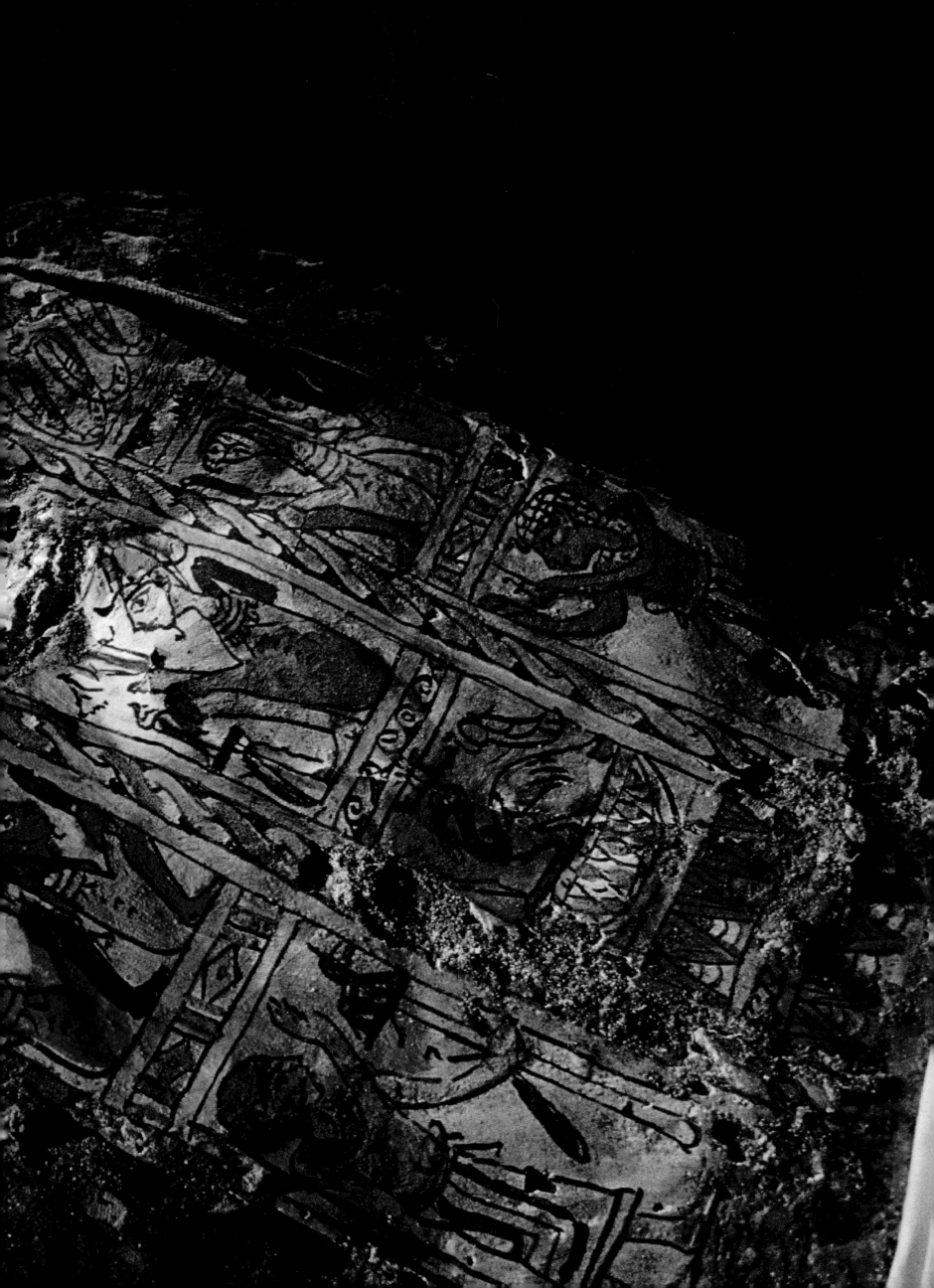

Adventurers and Explorers

Jean-François Champollion

Giovanni Battista Belzoni

Johann Ludwig Burckhardt

Henri Mouhot

John Lloyd Stephens
and Frederick Catherwood

Hiram Bingham

There is a fine line between a great adventurer and a great archaeologist. Both delight in their ability to explore uncharted deserts, jungles, mountains, and waters, all while fighting off local wildlife, dodging disease, and uncovering ancient ruins. Over the past century, however, the distinction has gradually evolved and the swashbuckling treasure-hunter has given rise to the hardcore scientist.

Today, truly great, adventurous archaeologists are defined not only by their ability to uncover history-altering remains of the past in remote locations, but also by the responsible manner in which they go about doing so.

That said, in this chapter, you'll read about some of the most inspiring early adventurers and explorers of all time, such as Ernest-Marc-Louis Doudart de Lagrée, who lost his own life as he documented the Mekong River, and John Lloyd Stephens and Frederick Catherwood, whose lavish descriptions and drawings brought Maya civilization out of the jungle and to the fingertips of the Western world through their bestselling volumes. Also included on these pages are Napoleon's "savants," who were sent to Egypt to record the country in encyclopedic fashion and returned with the Rosetta Stone, and Swiss traveler Johann Ludwig Burckhardt, whose fluency in Arabic led him to the forgotten city of Petra.

Perhaps the greatest adventurer-archaeologist of them all, however, is the fictional movie character Indiana Jones, who first ignited the silver screen in *Raiders of the Lost Ark* (1981). The world watched over the decades as he used a machete to hack through dense vegetation in Peru, piloted a plane out of Shanghai, and braved rat-infested catacombs in Venice. Recently, he even encountered extraterrestrial beings with crystal skulls that jetted off in a temple-turned-spacecraft.

The rugged and endearing professor of archaeology became equally admired for this suave look: the half-shaven, fedora-wearing, whip-carrying scoundrel who always got the girl. Who wouldn't want to be Indiana Jones? The dashing character had such an impact on interest in the study of archaeology that in 2009 the Archaeological Institute of America (AIA) elected Harrison Ford, the actor who played him, to its board of directors. "Knowledge is power," commented Ford, "and understanding the past can only help us in dealing with the present and the future."

But Indiana Jones is more than a figment of filmmaker George Lucas's wild imagination. He is believed to be an amalgamation of several actual archaeologists, adventurers, and explorers, including James Henry Breasted, the first American Egyptologist and founder of the University of Chicago's Oriental Institute. Breasted spent the majority of his 1895 honeymoon in Egypt acquiring artifacts for the institute's fledgling museum, which he kept in the couple's Nile riverboat suite. In a letter to her family, his new bride, Frances Hart, wrote:

"I was home by three—had lunch—and afterwards a good scrub. Then I made room for the products of our explorations. And lay down to rest and wait for husband. He came about 4:30 as well as the things and we had a great time, storing them in our small quarters. We had to take the dirty stuff in for fear of it being detected and taken. The back deck was filled so that we could not shut the door—and our dressing room was a pretty sight! We had to lean over a mummy case in order to wash in the morning and when I came to look for my tramping shoes, I finally discovered them under it!"

Indy's adventurous spirit can be seen throughout this entire volume, but two individuals outlined in this chapter have been repeatedly cited as sources of inspiration for the character: Hiram Bingham, who rediscovered Machu Picchu, the so-called "Lost City of the Incas," and Giovanni Battista Belzoni, a circus strongman who pillaged Egyptian tombs and temples.

Despite Harrison Ford's recognition by the AIA, not all archaeologists sing Indy's praises. Those who have devoted their lives to the discipline and to mastering the intricacies of scientific excavation techniques, meticulous documentation, and timely publication, call him a looter, plunderer, and treasure-hunter.

After all, he is not once seen documenting the context of a find. In the opening scene of *Raiders*, he famously exchanges a sack of sand for a golden idol, which he tucks inside his satchel as he dodges ancient booby traps, barely escaping with his life.

And as the great Treasury of Petra crumbles behind him in the final scene of *The Last Crusade* (1989), he makes one more attempt to pluck the Holy Grail from a perilous ledge as he risks being swallowed up by the trembling earth. But through his exploits, he genuinely risks life and limb to keep artifacts out of the hands of bad guys because they "belong in a museum."

Many, therefore, forgive his imperfections and embrace the romance that his character embodies—and, for the most part, his good intentions—alongside these early adventurers and explorers.

Their later modern counterparts can relate through their shared passion for travel, adventure, and, of course, discovery. Today, we are all too painfully aware of the importance of archaeological contexts and how they provide richness to the finds and their interpretation that is unattainable through a mere leather satchel full of shiny gold.

In the past couple of decades there have been advances in technology that these early adventurers and explorers couldn't possibly have imagined. With GIS mapping software, we can pinpoint exactly where to dig without touching the ground. With advanced CT scanners, we can look inside sealed mummy cases without peeling away a single fragment of a delicate *cartonnage*. With 3-D laser scanning, we can digitally document our entire ancient landscape, from Maya pyramids to Moai sculptures.

A computer technician working a continent away can meld images to re-create an ancient landscape and virtually excavate a site from their laptops, which launches them on a whole other kind of adventure. While today's archaeological pioneers brave an entirely new frontier, the spirit of the individuals discussed in this chapter inspired many of us to fall in love with the field and, hopefully, will continue to serve as sources of inspiration—and for some, perhaps, cautionary tales—for generations to come.(EBM)

Route de Paris a Syene
N.º 1167 milles 340.

Jean-François Champollion:
Napoleon's Army and Hieroglyphs, the Rosetta Stone

Jean-François Champollion's decipherment of Egyptian hieroglyphs proves that great disasters can lead to great discoveries. Napoleon's attempt to capture Egypt, giving France control of a key link between Europe and Asia, failed miserably. Just 20 days after he landed at Alexandria on July 1, 1798, Napoleon defeated the Egypt's Mameluke rulers in battle near the Giza pyramids. Before the battle he rallied his men, saying "Push on and recollect that from the summit of those monuments 40 centuries watch over us." Napoleon's triumph was brief. On August 1st, the British Admiral Nelson caught the French fleet at Aboukir Bay, east of Alexandria, and destroyed it.

Despite this setback, Napoleon remained in control of Egypt. His expedition of 55,000 men included 165 "savants"—scientists, engineers, surveyors, and artists—selected to gather information. The savants went about their research, eventually compiling the encyclopedic *Description de l'Égypte*. But Napoleon returned to France in August 1799, and two years later his army—cut off and decimated by plague—surrendered to the British. Under the terms, the savants' collections were forfeited.

Among the objects seized was the Rosetta Stone, an inscribed 1700-lb (762-kg) slab of stone discovered at the Nile Delta port of el-Rashid when foundations of a fort were being strengthened in 1799. The mundane text praises the pharaoh Ptolemy V for lowering the taxes on priests—but it was repeated in Greek, Demotic (Egyptian for daily use), and hieroglyphics (Egyptian for official and religious use). The French scholars had recognized the importance of the stone in deciphering ancient Egyptian writing. Even as King George III donated the stone to British Museum in 1802, work on the decipherment was underway.

Credit for the decipherment belongs to Jean-François Champollion. Born in southern France in 1790, he had a gift for languages, learning Greek and Latin at an early age. In 1801, he went to Grenoble and joined his older brother Jacques-Joseph, who had been in Egypt with Napoleon. At the same time, he met the mathematician Jean-Baptiste Fourier, one of leading savants and author of introduction to the *Description de l'Égypte*. And Champollion received a copy of the *Courrier de l'Égypte* that included an account of the Rosetta Stone's discovery.

Many scholars were already working on the Rosetta Stone inscriptions. Silvestre de Sacy urged comparison of the Greek and Demotic, especially looking for names in the Demotic corresponding to the ones in Greek, which could be read. The Swedish diplomat Johan David Åkerblad likewise focused on names. There was a general assumption that Demotic was alphabetic, while hieroglyphs were ideographic. But Georg Zoëga suggested some hieroglyphs might be phonetic, established how to determine the direction of the hieroglyphic writing, and maintained that cartouches were likely either religious formulas or names. Cartouches, named after the French word for cartridge, which Napoleon's soldiers thought they resembled, were in fact the names of Egyptian kings and queens.

As others did, Champollion attacked the decipherment by looking at names. The British scholar Thomas Young had identified the name of Ptolemy. Champollion added Cleopatra, which meant that he had a base of 12 known hieroglyphic letters. More and more evidence was becoming available to Champollion. The *Description de l'Égypte* volumes were coming out, and in September 1822 he received a consignment of drawings from a French architect who traveled in Egypt. Starting with his base of 12 known hieroglyphs, Champollion pinned down the names of Roman emperors and wives, as well as the preclasical pharaohs Ramses and Thutmosis. In September 1822, Champollion wrote his account of breaking the hieroglyphic code in his *Lettre à M. Dacier* (Dacier was secretary of the French Académie). By January 1823, Champollion had gone from the evidence of the Rosetta Stone to deciphering the names of some 30 pharaohs. The dead language, thanks to Champollion, could be read again. (MR)

Quelques images d'Oiseaux reçoivent aussi, parfois, une teinte rouge sur quelques unes de leurs parties ;

Et le Signe représentant un Oiseau qui vient de Naître totalement dénué de plumes est peint tout entier de couleur Rouge:

21 Les Hiéroglyphes sculptés en grand et figurant des Ustensiles, des instruments et objets de Costume prennent une couleur indiquant la matière dont ils sont formés:

Les objets en bois sont peints en Jaune :

(1)

La couleur Verte est donnée aux ustensiles en Bronze.

Il n'en est point ainsi pour les hiéroglyphes peints sur les monuments d'un petit Volume : on ne suit à cet égard aucune règle constante, beaucoup de caractère de cet ordre sont peints en en Verd en bleu ou en rouge indifféremment.

(1) un arc, une barque, une hache, une charrue, une paire de Sandales,

---

192 Soldiers from Napoleon's army marked their arrival in Aswan (Syene) by leaving an inscription on an ancient Egyptian monument. The scene is from an 1812 painting by Jean-Charles Tardieu (Versailles).

194 and 195 Jean-François Champollion's brother published his Egyptian grammar posthumously in 1836. The man who deciphered hieroglyphics had passed away in 1832, at the age of 41.

195 The Rosetta Stone bears a decree from Ptolemy V (196 B.C.) and was the final, though not the only, key to Champollion's decipherment of hieroglyphs (British Museum, London).

They surveyed it despite the torrid heat, finding large Osiris pillars sculpted in stone and detailed reliefs on the temple walls, but it was not the treasure they longed for.

After the first inspection of the Abu Simbel temple, the tireless Belzoni returned to Luxor. He wanted to explore the Valley of the Kings, where he'd already uncovered the tomb of the pharaoh Ay (18th Dynasty) in 1816. While digging in the valley, Belzoni's men came across the entrance to an unknown tomb on October 18, 1817. He had just found the burial place of Seti I (KV17), one of the largest and most lavishly decorated tombs in the Valley of the Kings. Belzoni wrote, "I may call this a fortunate day, one of the best perhaps in my life…[fortune] has given me that satisfaction, that extreme pleasure, which wealth cannot purchase; the pleasure of discovering what has been long sought in vain, and of presenting the world with a new and perfect monument of Egyptian antiquity." He traced some of the paintings in the tomb and removed portions to be sent to major European museums, which was a common practice at the time. The tomb of Seti I is still known as "Belzoni's tomb."

But his fame was destined to grow even more, when the enterprising adventurer decided to search the inner chambers of the Khafre pyramid at Giza. In terms of size, the pyramid of the 4th Dynasty pharaoh was second only to that of Khufu. It was explored by an Arab traveler in the 13th century, but no one had ventured into the heart of the monument since. Belzoni was successful in this undertaking as well, and on March 2, 1818, he entered the burial chamber by torchlight and breathed in the stale air, unaltered for centuries. As was the custom, Belzoni carved his name and the date inside the burial chamber, permanently marking his discovery.

Belzoni would go on to lead other expeditions in Egypt and make even more discoveries: identifying the Ptolemaic port of Berenice Troglodytica on the coast of the Red Sea; recovering an obelisk from the island of Philae; and being the first European to see the Bahariyah Oasis. In 1819, he left Egypt and returned to Europe, where he recorded his adventures in the land of the pharaohs, publishing the book *Narrative of the Operations and Recent Discoveries within the Pyramids, Temples, Tombs, and Ex-*

201 top The pyramid of Khafre, a 4th Dynasty pharaoh, is the second largest at Giza. Belzoni explored the inside for the first time in 1818.

201 bottom Belzoni chose to commemorate his efforts on a wall inside the funeral chamber of the Khafre pyramid. He wrote, "Discovered by G. Belzoni, March 2, 1818."

cavations, in Egypt and Nubia. Exhibits were organized in London and Paris, and the important artifacts that Belzoni had uncovered throughout his four years of work in Egypt were presented to the public.

A controversial figure, adventurous and romantic, obstinate and enterprising, Belzoni left his mark on the history of Egyptology in an era when the discipline had not yet become a science. He died on November 3, 1823, in a small village of Benin, while trying to complete the latest adventurous challenge of his life: exploring the legendary city of Timbuktu. (GF)

202-203 top The tomb of Seti I (KV 17), a 19th Dynasty pharaoh, contained splendid examples of wall paintings. Belzoni found it on October 18, 1817, while exploring the Valley of the Kings.

202-203 bottom Belzoni attributed the magnificent tomb found in the Valley of the Kings to Psammuthis, a pharaoh we now properly call Seti I. It is still referred to as "Belzoni's tomb."

204 top Though they were visited by Johan Ludwig Burckhardt in 1813 and John Bankes in 1815, the rock-cut temples at Abu Simbel had never been entered by Europeans. Belzoni became the first to do so on August 1, 1817, having finally removed all the sand blocking the entrance.

204 bottom and 205 Belzoni drew the large Osiris pillars holding up the hypostyle hall ceiling in the Great Temple at Abu Simbel. He was the first explorer to enter the monument after centuries of oblivion.

Haroun

Terrace
of Haroun

About A. is a large Temple similar to the
Kasır Faraoun. It was discovered at a distance
by Mʳ W. Bankes, Mʳ Legh, the Hon. Capt. Irby, and
Capt. Mangles, but circumstances did not admit
of their examining it. Ed.

A

Zob Faraoun

Ruins

Kasır Bent Faraoun

of

the

Tow

Wady Mousa

Sepulchres

Theatre

Sepulchres

Kasır Fa

EL SYK

Plan

of the Lower Parts of

WADY MOUSA.

Travels in Arabia:
Burckhardt and the Caravan City of Petra

John Lewis Burckhardt, one of the greatest travelers of his day, never attained his goal of exploring the interior of Africa. Instead, his fame lies in his explorations of Arabia, journey up the Nile to Nubia, daring pilgrimage to Mecca, and, above all, the discovery of the ancient city of Petra. Burckhardt was born in 1874 in Lausanne, Switzerland (he used the Anglicized version of his name, Johann Ludwig), and studied at Leipzig and Göttingen. In 1806, he moved to London, having a letter of introduction from one of his professors to Sir Joseph Banks, president of the Royal Society and a leader of the African Association.

Burckhardt was taken on by the Association to explore the African interior, traveling from the north. To prepare himself, he studied Arabic, natural sciences, and medicine at Cambridge and undertook long journeys on foot, sleeping on the ground and living on a diet of vegetables and water. In March 1809, Burckhardt left England for Malta en route to Aleppo, where he was to complete his mastery of the language and learn Arab customs. He adopted Arab garb and took the name Sheikh Ibrahim Ibn Abdallah. To mask his initially uncertain knowledge, he claimed to be a Muslim Indian returning from Europe: "Whenever I was asked for a specimen of the Hindu language, I answered in the worst dialect of the Swiss German, almost unintelligible even to a German, and which, in its guttural sounds, may fairly rival the harshest utterance of Arabic."

He traveled widely, visiting Palmyra, Damascus, and Lebanon. In the summer of 1812, he journeyed toward Cairo, intending to join a caravan to Fezzan, and from there explore the sources of the Niger. From Damascus he went through the mountains of Arabia Petræa in what is now Jordan. There, he heard locals speak with great admiration of some ancient ruins and he went to investigate them, a somewhat delicate operation: "I knew well the character of the people around me; I was without protection in the midst of a desert where no traveler had ever before been seen; and a close examination of these works of the infidels, as they are called, would have excited suspicions that I was a magician in search of treasures."

What he found was Petra, the capital of the Nabataeans. The Nabataean kingdom rose to prominence toward the close of the 2nd century B.C., buoyed by its control of trade routes. From Petra, these extended west to Gaza, north to Basra and Damascus, south to the Red Sea port Aqaba, and across Arabia to the Persian Gulf. Petra itself was a cosmopolitan city, with Greek, Egyptian, and Syrian elements as well as native Nabataean ones.

In a letter to the African Association sent from Cairo, sent September 12, Burckhardt described the vast ruins:

"This place is very interesting for its antiquities and the remains of an ancient city, which I conjecture to be Petra, the capital of Arabia Petraea, a place which, as far as I know, no European traveler has ever visited. In the red sand stone of which the valley is composed, are upwards of 250 sepulchers entirely cut out of rock, the greater part of them with Grecian ornaments. There is a mausoleum in the shape of a temple, of colossal dimensions, likewise cut out of the rock, with all its apartments, its vestibule, peristyle, &c. It is a most beautiful specimen of Grecian architecture, and in perfect preservation. There are other mausolea with obelisks, apparently in the Egyptian style, a whole amphitheatre cut out of the rock with the remains of a palace and of several temples."

However, Petra's age of glory was brief. In A.D. 106, the region was absorbed into the Roman Empire as part of the province Arabia Petræa. For a while, Petra flourished, but over the next century, the trade routes shifted and Palmyra grew in importance. An earthquake in A.D. 363 damaged many building in Petra and disrupted its water-supply system, a critical blow from which the desert city never recovered.

In Cairo, Burckhardt found that no Fezzan caravan was imminent, so he traveled up the Nile into Nubia. Finding it impossible to penetrate westward into the African interior, he crossed the Nubian desert disguised as a poor Syrian merchant, and reached Suakin on the Red Sea. From there he performed the pilgrimage to Mecca, where he stayed three months. It was only in 1817 that he resumed preparations for his journey into the African interior, but in Cairo he was seized with dysentery and died on October 15. (MR)

206 Burckhardt made this Wadi Musa map in 1812, depicting the ruins of the ancient Nabataean capital. The topographic development isn't completely accurate, but it shows the names of the major monuments.

208 Burckhardt's travels were sponsored by the British Association for Promoting the Discovery of the Interior Parts of Africa. He recorded his discoveries in several diaries, which are now valuable sources of information.

208-209 Carved into the rock of the Jebel al-Khubtha in the center of Petra, the Royal Tombs are among the largest and most elegantly crafted burial sites in the Nabataean city.

210 The monuments in the Nabataean city discovered by Burckhardt were made famous to the Western public through the beautiful lithographs of English landscape artist David Roberts, who visited Petra in 1839. Here the artist depicts the site's most celebrated monument, the Khazneh al-Faroun ("Pharaoh's Treasury"). This magnificent rock tomb appears to visitors upon exiting the Siq, the narrow and evocative passage leading into the city.

211 The face of the Khazneh al-Faroun is illuminated by the sun, in stark contrast to the shadows cast by the vertical rock walls of the Siq. This is where Hellenistic architecture blends with the Eastern tastes of the Nabataean civilization.

212-213 Petra's largest monument is Ed-Deir ("The Monastery"), whose solid form and strong lines emerge from a rock mass at the summit of a cliff. Like the Khazneh al-Faraoun, it must have been the tomb of an elite individual.

214-215 David Roberts wrote about his visit to Ed-Deir in his diary: "We wound our way up a steep ravine; a broken staircase extending the whole ascent… We at length reached the object of our journey, which was a building rarely visited, called Ed-Deir (The Monastery). It is hewn out of the face of the rock… Though the ruins of this extraordinary place are immense, they sink into insignificance when compared with these stupendous rocks."

215 This lithograph by Roberts captures the carved rock facades of the Royal Tombs of Petra in all their glory: the Urn Tomb, the Silk Tomb, the Corinthian Tomb, and the Palace Tomb.

Explorers on the Mekong River:
Angkor Rediscovered

The jungle-covered sandstone ruins of the ancient city of Angkor in Cambodia were well known to the people who lived nearby as well as a handful of Portuguese travelers, a French missionary, and even a Japanese pilgrim who wrote about the site some 200 years after its abandonment in the 15th century A.D. But it wasn't until French naturalist and explorer Alexandre-Henri Mouhot—who visited Angkor in 1860 while investigating the Mekong River's tributaries on an expedition with the British Royal Geographic Society—published vivid descriptions and lavish pen-and-ink sketches of its sprawling temple complex and lotus-shaped towers that the West became fascinated with this mysterious "lost" city.

In June 1866, a French team launched the first formal expedition to document the Mekong River and to see if it would be navigable all the way to China so new trade routes could be established. Led by two naval officers, Commander Ernest-Marc-Louis Doudart de Lagrée and Lieutenant Francis Garnier, the team of two-dozen men included fellow explorers and interpreters, as well as French and Filipino soldiers, and Vietnamese militiamen. While treacherous rapids and falls, including the Khone Falls near the border of Cambodia and Laos, prevented the mission's economic success, the team's careful mapping of 4,200 miles (6,700 km) of the Mekong's twists, turns, and environs cemented its importance in history. The party famously also stopped at Angkor to study and record its ruins before continuing its journey. Unfortunately, Doudart de Lagrée did not live to see Garnier's 1873 publication of the expedition, *Voyage d'exploration en Indochine* (*Voyage of Exploration in Indochina*), which is still an invaluable volume to researchers today. Suffering from ulcers, fever, infected wounds, and dysentery, he died along the way in March 1868. Garnier therefore took over command for the expedition's final three months. Doudart de Lagrée was buried in Dongchuan, China, but his heart was removed and returned to his native France.

One member of the expedition, Louis Delaporte, later returned to further document the site. Artwork from Angkor, which he shipped back to France, also inspired Parisian architect Lucien Fournereau to visit in 1887 and create fantastic plans and cross sections. In 1902, a group of archaeologists and philologists under the name École Française d'Extrême Orient (EFEO) began work at the site. In 1907, Angkor, then under Thai control, was returned to Cambodia, and the EFEO became responsible for mapping, restoring, and maintaining the site, as well as opening it up to tourists. Today, the Greater Angkor Project (GAP) uses advanced technology, including NASA radar imagery and remote-sensing applications, to study it. Recent research has revealed an extensive waterworks system and expansive hydraulic network, and has suggested that the entire city once covered some 390 sq miles (1000 sq km) and may have housed a population of around 750,000 at its height in the 12th or 13th century.

The city of Angkor was built by the mighty Khmer Empire that once controlled most of Southeast Asia. It became the capital of the empire in the 9th century A.D. but reached its greatest height between the 12th and 15th centuries. While the vast complex is made up of hundreds of structures and monuments, there are two particularly fantastic ones that have most captivated the world's attention. The 215-ft (65-m) high lotus-shaped towers of Angkor Wat, the 12th-century temple-mausoleum of King Suryavarman II, mark the final resting place of the ruler as well as the residence of the Hindu god Vishnu.

Believed to have taken some 30 years to complete, the splendid structure was built without any mortar; elephants were used to fit its heavy sandstone blocks into place.

216   In the late 19th century, French explorer Louis Delaporte documented the site of Angkor, which was designated
a UNESCO World Heritage site in 1992.

218-219   Detailed sketches of Angkor from French naturalist Mouhot's 1863 visit were published
in his *Le tour du monde: Nouveau journal des voyages* (1868).

219   Although many knew of Angkor's existence, Mouhot was posthumously anointed its discoverer little more
than a decade after his trip.

Also of particular renown is Angkor Thom, a fortified temple complex built by King Jayavarman VII around A.D. 1200 to protect the people who lived there from raids by the Cham from the area of modern-day Vietnam. The identity of the colossal heads that define its 75-ft (23-m) tall stone towers remains a mystery, but many scholars believe they represent the bodhisattva Avalokiteshvara facing the four cardinal directions.

Following a major battle in 1431 with the Kingdom of Siam, Angkor was abandoned. Scholars now argue that overuse of the surrounding rice fields, deforestation, and overpopulation were also to blame for the downfall of the city that had thrived over the course of 500 years and 22 kings. (EBM)

220-221 The great temple-mausoleum of Angkor Wat is surrounded by a moat that runs 3.5 miles (5.5 km) around its perimeter and is crossable in only two places. Shown here is the west approach, a 660-ft (200-m) long, 40-ft (12-m) wide causeway paved with sandstone.

222-223 This Delaporte sketch shows the fortified city of Angkor Thom, through which an elaborate water system ran along its north-south axis.

223 In 1866, Ernest-Marc-Louis Doudart de Lagrée led a French expedition to chart the Mekong River. Although he died along the way, his team successfully completed the journey under Lieutenant Francis Garnier.

224-225 Some believe Angkor Thom's towers depict the bodhisattva Avalokiteshvara facing the four cardinal directions. Others argue that they represent guardians of the site or even Jayavarman VII, the ruler who undertook its construction.

Stephens and Catherwood:
Exploring the Maya Jungle

Few collaborations have had as much impact as the explorations and publications by American John Lloyd Stephens (1805–1852) and Englishman Frederick Catherwood (1799–1854). In the words of one eminent Mayanist, they "literally opened up the field of Maya archaeology."

Their books, *Incidents of Travel in Central America, Chiapas and Yucatán* (1841) and *Incidents of Travel in Yucatán* (1843), describe how they, "discovered the crumbling remains of 44 ancient cities…with but few exceptions, all were lost, buried, and unknown, never before visited by a stranger." The text, by Stephens, not only provided the first reliable accounts of many of the sites, but also insights and ethnographic notes about the Indians. With the notes are engravings made from original art by Catherwood, much of it created using a camera lucida, which projected the image onto paper in which it could be traced very accurately and with extraordinary detail.

Stephens studied law and entered into practice in New York City, but after an illness he was advised to take a sea voyage for his health. In 1834, he began two years of travel, writing about his journeys and the peoples and ancient monuments he saw in *Incidents of Travel in Egypt, Arabia Petraea, and the Holy Land* (1837) and *Incidents of Travel in Greece, Turkey, Russia, and Poland* (1838). Between 1824 and 1832, Frederick Catherwood, who was trained as an architect at Cambridge, traveled throughout the Mediterranean, to the Levant, and to Egypt making drawings and watercolors of the ruins.

They met in London in 1836, and discussed traveling together to see and record ancient sites in Central America. That came about three years later. Their first major site, which they arrived at late in 1839, was Copán (in what is today Honduras): "We…ascended [the pyramid] by regular stone steps, which in some places had been forced apart by bushes and saplings and in others

thrown down by the growth of large trees. In parts they were ornamented with sculptured figures and rows of death's heads. Climbing over the ruined top, we reached a terrace overgrown with trees."

They continued on, seeing and recording major sites in Mexico such as Palenque (Chiapas) and Uxmal (Yucatán). On their second expedition they returned to Uxmal, but also documented ruins at many other famous sites in Yucatán including Tulum, Chichén Itzá, Mayapan, and Kabah. For Mesoamerica, the works of Stephens and Catherwood begin what scholars refer to as Classificatory-Descriptive Period. Their books set the standard for publications in terms of making a thorough assessment of these newly discovered sites, even if the interpretation of the remains was somewhat limited. They did, however, come to some very important conclusions.

The first conclusion was the age of the Maya sites was measurable in centuries rather than millennia: "It perhaps destroys much of the interest that hangs over these ruins to assign to them a modern date; but we live in an age whose spirit is to discard phantasms and arrive at truth."

This meant that the early colonial government and church archives—largely untouched by archaeological scholars—might hold valuable information about the Maya civilization. Stephens argued that investigation of such historical documents was as important as finding more sites or deciphering the glyphs.

The second conclusion was that the Maya civilization had an "independent existence." The Maya were not inspired by or derived from some other Old World culture or lost race, and they were the forebears of the living Indians:

"In identifying [the ruins] as the works of the ancestors of the present Indians, the cloud which hung over their origin is not removed; the time when and the circumstances under which they were built, the rise, the progress, and full development of the

226 This lithograph by Frederick Catherwood depicts Stela H at Copán, the Maya site in Honduras, which he visited with John Stephens in 1839. The monument was completely covered in tropical vegetation when it was first discovered, and it had to be cleared away to create the image.

228-229 Workers hired by Stephens and Catherwood clear ruins at Tulum. Catherwood appears in the center-right, measuring the temple.

229 Catherwood's drawing of the "Nunnery," a Puuc-style masterpiece in the Yucatan city of Chichén Itzá.

power, art, and skill required for their construction, are all mysteries which will not be easily unraveled. They rise like skeletons from the grave, wrapped in their burial shrouds."

Incidents of Travel in Central America and *Incidents of Travel in Yucatán* has remained in print for more than a 150 years thanks to Catherwood's artistic abilities and to Stephens' writing, which could be simultaneously evocative and intellectual. Stephens also had a gift for observation, reporting everything he saw around him even if it reflected on him and Catherwood in an unflattering light, such as their being unable to light a campfire at Uxmal, even with the aid of gunpowder.

But they did not continue their great collaboration. Stephens went into business, first helping to launch the Ocean Steam Navigation Company in an attempt to break into the transatlantic passenger trade, then with the Panama Railroad Company. In traveling to Bogotá, Stephens injured his back badly when his mule fell. His health never fully recovered and he died in 1850. Catherwood became a merchant in the California Gold Rush trade center of San Francisco. He died in 1854, after SS *Arctic*, the ship in which he was sailing to England, collided with another vessel in the mid-Atlantic and sank. (MR)

230-231 The great "el Castillo" pyramid, a temple to Kukulkan (feathered serpent) in Chichen Itza, is still partially covered in the lush Yucatan vegetation depicted in this Catherwood drawing.

Hiram Bingham:
The Lost City of the Inca Empire

The adventurous Yale University professor Hiram Bingham is one of the most famous archaeologists of the 20th century, not only because he is widely credited with rediscovering Peru's Machu Picchu, the Lost City of the Incas, but also because he served as one of the sources of inspiration for the legendary Indiana Jones movie character. Today, however, Bingham and his great discovery remain shrouded in controversy, and the artifacts he brought back from the site for display in Yale's museum are at the center of an intense international debate over their ownership. The exciting story of this real-life dashing explorer of South American archaeology, still making headlines more than five decades after his death, would even make his Hollywood counterpart tip his fedora.

In 1906–07, Bingham led an expedition in the footsteps of an 1819 journey taken by Simón Bolívar, the leader of Peru between 1823 and 1826, who had followed an old Spanish trade route from Buenos Aires to Lima. The history teacher had been hoping to expand his knowledge of Latin America to share with his students. But upon arriving in Cusco, the ancient capital of the Inca Empire, Bingham became intrigued with tales he had heard of Vilcabamba, the "last resting place of the Incas," which had fallen to the Spanish in 1573.

Fascinated with the idea of finding and exploring this last Inca stronghold, he returned to Peru in July of 1911 with the Yale Peruvian Scientific Expedition and the financial support of Yale University and the National Geographic Society. With the help of 17th-century writings and a local policeman as a guide, the small team set out on foot and mule. But it was a tip about impressive nearby ruins from a local farmer named Melchor Arteaga that helped guide the expedition on a two-day ascent up the Andean mountain. Upon reaching the top, Bingham later wrote in his 1948 bestseller *Lost City of the Incas*:

"Suddenly I found myself confronted with the walls of ruined houses built of the finest quality of Inca stonework. It was hard to see them for they were partly covered with trees and moss, the growth of centuries, but in the dense shadow, hiding in bamboo thickets and tangled vines, appeared here and there walls of white granite ashlars carefully cut and exquisitely fitted together.... I climbed a marvelous great stairway of large granite blocks, walked along a pampa where the Indians had a small vegetable garden, and came into a little clearing. Here were the ruins of two of the finest structures I have ever seen in Peru. Not only were they made of selected blocks of beautifully grained white granite; their walls contained ashlars of Cyclopean size, 10 feet in length, and higher than a man. The sight held me spellbound.... I could scarcely believe my senses as I examined the larger blocks in the lower course, and estimated that they must weigh from 10 to 15 tons each. Would anyone believe what I had found?"

Bingham excavated for two seasons (1911–12 and 1914–15), during which he also photographed and documented site, which he initially believed to be the legendary Vilcabamba, an interpretation supported by many until the mid-20th century. (Today, scholars understand Machu Picchu, built in the 1400s and in use until the arrival of the Spanish more than a century later, mainly to have been the summer highland retreat of Inca royalty.) Even more important, however, he brought Machu Picchu to the world's attention through publications such as the April 1913 issue of *National Geographic*, which was entirely devoted to the find.

A romantic figure, Bingham's image has been tarnished over the years, as mounting evidence—including maps that pinpoint the site as early as 1874—has surfaced and pointed to other foreign visitors who may have reached Machu Picchu first, including British missionary Thomas Payne, who lived in Peru from 1903 to 1952, and German engineer J. M. von Hassel who passed through the area in 1910. Recently, some have claimed that German adventurer Augsto Berns not only got there first, in 1867, but in the 1880s

232 Born in Honolulu, Hawaii, Hiram Bingham received his M.A. from the University of California at Berkley and his Ph.D. from Yale in Latin American history.

234 top On his first trip to South America, Bingham followed an old Spanish trade route from Buenos Aires to Lima.

234 bottom In 1911, Bingham set out with a team of seven men on the Yale Peruvian Scientific Expedition to find Vilcabamba, the legendary last Inca stronghold.

235 Bingham's team traveled by foot and donkey, often through treacherous snake-infested pathways up the Andean mountain.

looted the site. Berns, who had moved to Peru in the 1860s to work on the Southern Peruvian Railway, spied Machu Picchu from the vantage point of nearby property he purchased some 20 years later, and upon which he built a sawmill while he raised money to strip it of its treasures, including gold and silver, supposedly with permission from the Peruvian government. Some argue that documents in Yale's archives point to evidence that Bingham may have known about Berns. The matter remains the subject of lively scholarly debate.

Even more disconcerting is the ongoing present-day battle between Yale and the government of Peru, which demands the return of more than 5,000 artifacts that Bingham brought back from his 1911–12 excavations and have been in the Peabody Museum of Natural History's collection at the university for nearly a century. (The Peruvian government's policy changed after 1912, and artifacts from Bingham's second 1914–15 expedition were loaned to the university museum and then returned after a delay attributed to World War I.) Peru cites a presidential decree permitting Bingham's excavations at Machu Picchu, which also allowed him to bring artifacts back to Yale for scientific study. "Unique" or "duplicate" artifacts, it states, would then be returned to Peru upon request.

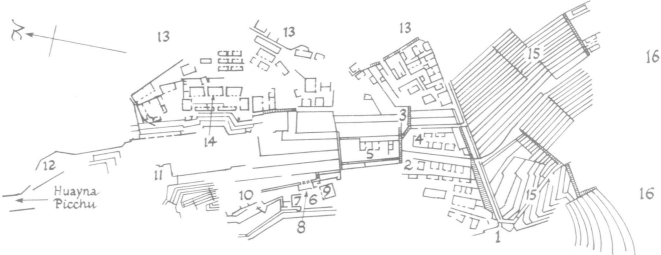

Yale interprets the agreement differently and contends it is legally in possession of the site's materials.

In September 2007, Yale and Peru signed a Memorandum of Understanding (MOU), which laid the groundwork for international collaboration in the artifacts' study and display, including a traveling exhibition as well as the creation of a new museum in Peru to house them. Unfortunately, negotiations broke down and in December 2008, Peru sued Yale for the objects' return, as well as for monetary damages, estimated to be upward of $75,000. A major development occurred in March 2010, when Peru withdrew allegations of fraud and conspiracy against the Ivy League institution—accusing Yale of deceiving Peru by pledging to return the artifacts—thus dismissing 6 of 17 counts from its 2008 lawsuit.

In 1948, the road from Cusco to Machu Picchu was christened the Hiram Bingham Highway, and Bingham was invited back to Peru for its dedication. According to a local newspaper, the Peruvian government's representative said that the highway would "again unite the prestige of the illustrious professor, Dr. Hiram Bingham, with the destiny of our country." For more than 60 years, tourists have been streaming in to see the site, which in 2007 was named one of the Modern Wonders of the World. While the future of its artifacts remains up in the air—along with the identity of the explorer who first glimpsed its spectacular ruins —it is certain that Bingham may be credited for introducing Machu Picchu to the world, and in so doing, imbuing the field of archaeology with a century's worth of marvelous tales and international intrigue. (EBM)

1. City Gate
2. Divided stairway and round tower over first cave
3. Stairway to the fountains
4. Royal Mausoleum
5. King's Group
6. Sacred Plaza
7. Principal Temple
8. Temple of the Three Windows
9. High Priest's House
10. Hutihuana Hill
11. Terraced gardens
12. Terraced gardens and sacrificial rocks
13. Main residential areas with terraces and burial caves below
14. Three-door group
15. Agricultural terraces
16. Steep hillside covered with rubble, probably former agricultural terraces

236-237 For decades, Bingham believed he had discovered Vilcabamba, but scholars ultimately concluded that Machu Picchu was used mainly as a summer retreat for Inca royalty. As it turns out, Bingham did come across the nearby site of Vilcabamba, which was only years later properly identified.

236 bottom Machu Picchu's complex layout once suggested to archaeologists that it may have been the site of a great city or sprawling temple complex, interpretations that have both been disproven.

237 Machu Picchu is sometimes described as the City in the Clouds, as it lies some 8,200 ft (2,500 m) above sea level. This photo was taken during the Bingham expedition.

Chance Discoveries

In its nascent years of adventurers and explorers, archaeological methodology left a lot to be desired, according to today's standards. Expeditions to far-flung corners of the globe were launched by men of means—or those who knew and had charmed such men with stories of ancient ruins and buried treasures—and very little was known in advance of what would be encountered in the heart of a jungle or the fringe of a desert. These early, pioneering "archaeologists" sought spectacular finds that would bring them fame and glory. There were still fantastic, unknown civilizations to be brought to light and lost cities to be rediscovered. And while they were undoubtedly instrumental in locating, exploring, and writing about these remote spots, they didn't always know what to do when they got there, and often irreparably damaged archaeological contexts as they searched for museum showpieces. Untold sites still slumber beneath the earth's surface, and archaeologists have since made great strides in piecing together our shared cultural heritage through the development of a sound, scientific approach to excavations.

These days, most great archaeological discoveries are the result of years of careful planning. First, the team may conduct a site survey. If the surface finds look promising, the researchers may begin the lengthy process of applying for permission to conduct further, sometimes digital investigations, to dig, and securing funding for the project. After laborious excavations, the team may start to establish a chronology through identifying and dating well-documented pottery types and studying the site's stratigraphy. Through extensive research, they may then begin to put together the site's pieces and determine its place in history by analyzing the finds, a job that may span entire careers, which is undertaken only by the most dedicated individuals. The resulting discoveries range from the fabulously unique to the commonplace, the latter more frequently surfacing.

Pottery is usually the most prevalent find and most valuable for dating purposes—though perhaps the least exciting. But through hard work, patience, and persistence, archaeologists are still uncovering a wide variety of finds.

For instance, after five years of scientific research and investigation, the world's oldest-known oil paintings were identified in caves along the Silk Road, covered with Buddhist art in Afghanistan's Bamiyan Valley. And after a quarter of a century of excavations at the Iron Age necropolis of Orthi Petra at Eleutherna on Crete, archaeologists have only begun to uncover the women who were buried there—surrounded by gold, silver, semiprecious stones, and in some cases, ritual implements for important religious ceremonies—which has started to illuminate their powerful role during the Dark Ages of Greece. Then, there is the Egyptian mummy Meresamun that was in the collection of the University of Chicago's Oriental Institute Museum for nearly 100 years before researchers were able to study her remains with advanced enough technology to learn more about her life and death. And after centuries of admiring ancient Greek and Roman sculpture for its exquisite simplicity—fashioned, as once believed, from plain white marble—scholars are only now beginning to fully absorb the results of extensive analysis that shows it was actually covered in vibrant paint.

Each of these discoveries is the result of intense scientific research that can take years, and even decades. Today, archaeology is indeed for the patient and serious scholar. So when a stray critter, vacationing amateur scuba diver, or local farmer makes an instantaneous "chance" discovery so extraordinary that a nation's history could barely be written without it, the archaeological community is collectively dumbfounded.

This is the case with each discovery detailed in this chapter. It is almost impossible to believe that a stray goat led its Bedouin herder to the Dead Sea Scrolls, the oldest-known copies of the Hebrew Bible. It is perhaps even more incredible that a chemist on holiday stumbled upon the finest extant examples of Greek bronze sculpture ever brought up from the seafloor. And who would have dreamed that farmers in the countryside of Shaanxi Province near Xi'an, China, would search for a place to dig a water well and instead find the 2,200-year-old terracotta army, thousands strong, of the country's notorious first emperor?

On the following pages, you'll also read about the mounds on the estate of an Englishwoman—inspired to have them excavated in the 1930s by a trip to Egypt—that yielded the glittering hoard of an Anglo-Saxon king. You'll also learn of the "Mindenhall Treasure," which consists of 34 Roman serving pieces of the 4th century A.D. date, and find out why its chance discovery by a farmer plowing his field remains shrouded in mystery. And then you'll be as baffled as the archaeologists to see how an amateur metal detectorist recently brought to light a 1,700-piece treasure—the most significant Anglo-Saxon hoard discovered to date.

Fortunately, there are still amazing finds waiting underground for an archaeologist's trowel, barely escaping their "chance" discovery. In 2008, for example, a team of archaeologists unearthed a magnificent, 800-lb (360-kg) 8th-century B.C. basalt stele at the site of Zincirli in southeastern Turkey. It depicts a high official named Kuttamuwa sipping wine and feasting on meat and bread at his own funerary banquet. Its 13-line inscription, written in a dialect called Sam'alian, talks about offerings that were made in his mortuary chapel, including "a ram for my soul that is in this stele." This singular line has helped illuminate Iron Age beliefs in the afterlife. Even though the body had been cremated, the soul—which was believed by surrounding cultures to inhabit one's bones—lived on in this massive stone. While it was scientifically excavated, the Kuttamuwa stele just barely escaped yet another chance discovery. It was unearthed a mere 8 in (20 cm) below the surface of a wheat field that had been farmed for generations. Although it is otherwise intact, its rounded top contains deep scratches from modern plows.

While it might be tempting for archaeologists to drop their trowels and take up farming—or trade in their GIS software for metal detectors (or a trusted goat)—these incredible finds still are the exceptions to the archaeological rule. Yet sound science and methodology combined with a healthy helping of chance and a dash of luck never hurt. (EBM)

The Mildenhall Treasure

Sometimes what appears to be the chance unearthing of ancient masterpieces involves deceit as well as discovery. This may be true for the Mildenhall Treasure—a buried hoard containing 34 pieces of 4th-century A.D. Roman plates and utensils—but we may never know.

The popular story is one of a "regular" person, Gordon Butcher, a plowman employed by one Sydney Ford, making a fantastic discovery. In January 1942, as the tale goes, Butcher was plowing a field in Mildenhall, Suffolk, owned by Fred Rolfe. Butcher ran the plow deeper than usual because the field was going to be planted with sugar beets and it hit a large silver dish.

Uncertain what to do, Butcher went to his boss, Ford, who was known to be an antiquarian. Together they unearthed the hoard. The largest piece was a 24-in (60.5-cm) diameter dish (18 lb/8.256 kg), decorated with scenes of the god Bacchus and Hercules, as well as Pan, drinking. On an inner band, sea-nymphs or nereids riding mythical marine creatures surround the head of Oceanus, who is depicted with dolphins in his hair and seaweed in his beard. A second large dish, 22 in (55.6 cm) in diameter, is decorated with geometric motifs in dark-colored niello (silver sulfide), contrasting with the polished silver surface. Other pieces included silver platters with Pan and maenads (the female followers of Bacchus), a covered bowl with centaurs and wild animals, flanged bowls, ladles, and spoons (three with Christian symbols, Chi-Rho and Alpha-Omega)

Ford, despite his reputation as an antiquarian, told Butcher he thought the pieces were of pewter, and took them all home. For the duration of the war, Ford unbent the pieces and cleaned them of corrosion. He kept some of them on his fireplace mantle, supposedly not recognizing their value.

In 1946, four years after the discovery, Dr. Hugh Fawcett, a Buckinghamshire member of Parliament and an antiquarian, visited Ford and saw some pieces of the treasure. Fawcett thought they were important and took some objects to the British Museum, where specialists identified them as 4th-century Roman silver. The treasure was acquired for the museum and put on display in July 1946.

Perhaps the Mildenhall Treasure was buried in the late 4th century, when Saxons threatened southeastern Britain, and was never recovered by its owner. But is that what really happened? None of the pieces show damage from the plow, which would be expected if Butcher's account is true. An excavation in July 1946 at the spot where Ford said the treasure was found revealed no pits or artifacts. There were suggestions it had been discovered elsewhere, perhaps in North Africa, and brought back surreptitiously by pilots using the air base at Mildenhall, near where it could be buried and later "found." Some have wondered, too, if Ford's taking of the treasure was entirely innocent, or if he sought to keep it all for himself, excluding Butcher. The answers to these questions may never be known.

Recently, concerns of another sort were raised. Did the British Museum acquire the entire treasure, or did Ford retain some of the objects? In 2002, 94-year-old Jack Thompson said that Ford had him clean a five-inch-high goblet with four legs. No such piece is in the museum's collection. Furthermore, a photograph taken between 1942 and 1946 appears to show another silver vessel, now unaccounted for, resting on Ford's mantle.

Undoubtedly the Mildenhall Treasure is one of late antiquity's greatest discoveries. There is speculation that it could even have belonged to Lupicinus, a general serving in Britain during the reign of the emperor Julian (A.D. 360–363). But some 70 years after it was found, the treasure remains shrouded in mystery. (MR)

242 The Great Dish from the Mildenhall Treasure is decorated with a Bacchic theme in relief (British Museum, London).

244-245 and 245 bottom Two silver plates from the Mildenhall Treasure feature a series of real and fantastic animals around the border. In the center medallion, a hunter faces a bear (British Museum, London).

245 top This photo of a family member was taken at the home of Sydney Ford. Some dishes from the Mildenhall Treasure are visible on the furniture in the background.

246-247 The cover of this bowl from the Mildenhall Treasure has a Bacchic design in relief around the border and a small triton statuette on top (British Museum, London).

247 These plates bear the recurring Bacchic theme that's present on many items from the Mildenhall Treasure. Two maenads dance and play music, accompanied by a satyr and the god Pan (British Museum, London).

Sutton Hoo:
An Anglo-Saxon Ship Burial

"What about this?" replied landowner Edith Pretty when asked where to dig by archaeologist Basil Brown. After visiting Egypt, Pretty became interested in archaeology. Her estate had several mounds on it and the preceding year, 1938, she had hired Brown to investigate them. The three mounds he dug into had been plundered, but still yielded tantalizing remains from wealthy burials: bronze vessel fragments, gilt bronze shield decorations, and a silver buckle and gilt silver drinking horn mount. So, Pretty continued in 1939, selecting the largest mound for that year's excavation.

Brown, removing the upper layers of the mound, found iron rivets and impressions of timber planks—the "ghost" of a 90-ft (27-m) long ship preserved in the sandy soil. At the center of the ship were the remains of a cabin possibly holding a burial. It was then excavated by specialists from Cambridge, who carefully uncovered what proved to be the undisturbed interment of an Anglo-Saxon king.

The early Anglo-Saxon period was thought to be a "Dark Age." Roman forces withdrew from Britain in A.D. 410, and by ca. A.D. 450 invading Angles, Saxons and Jutes crossed the North Sea and took over eastern and central England. By the late 6th century, they had established seven kingdoms: Mercia, Northumbria, East Angles (Norfolk), East Angles (Suffolk), Wessex, Kent, and Sussex. Accounts of their constant petty wars in the *Anglo-Saxon Chronicle* and the *Ecclesiastical History of Bede* gave the impression of a step back to barbarianism from the preceding, civilized ways of the Romano-British. That was the perception before Sutton Hoo, but the find led to a radical change in the appreciation of artistry and wealth of the Anglo-Saxons.

The king had gone to the grave with his elaborately decorated helmet, chain-mail armor, a formidable ax-hammer, spears, sword, and shield. The helmet has tinned bronze foil panels decorated with interlacing animal ornament and heroic scenes; the sword has a gold and garnet pommel, gold guards, and filigree clips on its hilt. The broad belt from which the sword hung had an immense, triangular buckle of gold (14.5 oz/412.7 gr) also decorated with intertwined animals. Hinged shoulder clasps of gold inlaid with garnets had held a leather overgarment.

The ruler's wealth and power were epitomized by a leather purse of which the jeweled lid remained and a unique object thought to be a scepter. The purse contained 37 Merovingian gold coins plus three blanks and two billets (the coins and blanks possibly for 40 oarsmen and the billets for the steersman to ferry the dead king to the afterlife). A long, four-sided whetstone, the "scepter" has carved faces and bronze fittings at each end, with a cast bronze stag (red deer) with antlers on top. Royal feasting and entertainment are attested by maplewood bottles, drinking horns, and walnut cups with silver and silver-gilt fittings; bronze hanging bowls and cauldrons; and a maplewood lyre with gilded bronze fittings and garnet settings. A bronze Coptic bowl and 16 silver pieces, including 28.5-in (72.4-cm) diameter dish, come from eastern Mediterranean workshops, likely via Europe to the Merovingians and on to Britain. Crosses and inscriptions on some of the silver pieces might be Christian references, but that is not certain.

The most likely identification of the man buried at Sutton Hoo is Raedwald, king of East Angles who died around A.D. 624–625. Raedwald's rich and beautifully crafted grave goods, as well as evidence of international connections, reflected a much less "dark" Anglo-Saxon period than had been assumed. The princely burial found at Prittlewell in 2003 and the newly discovered Staffordshire hoard have brightened it even more. (MR)

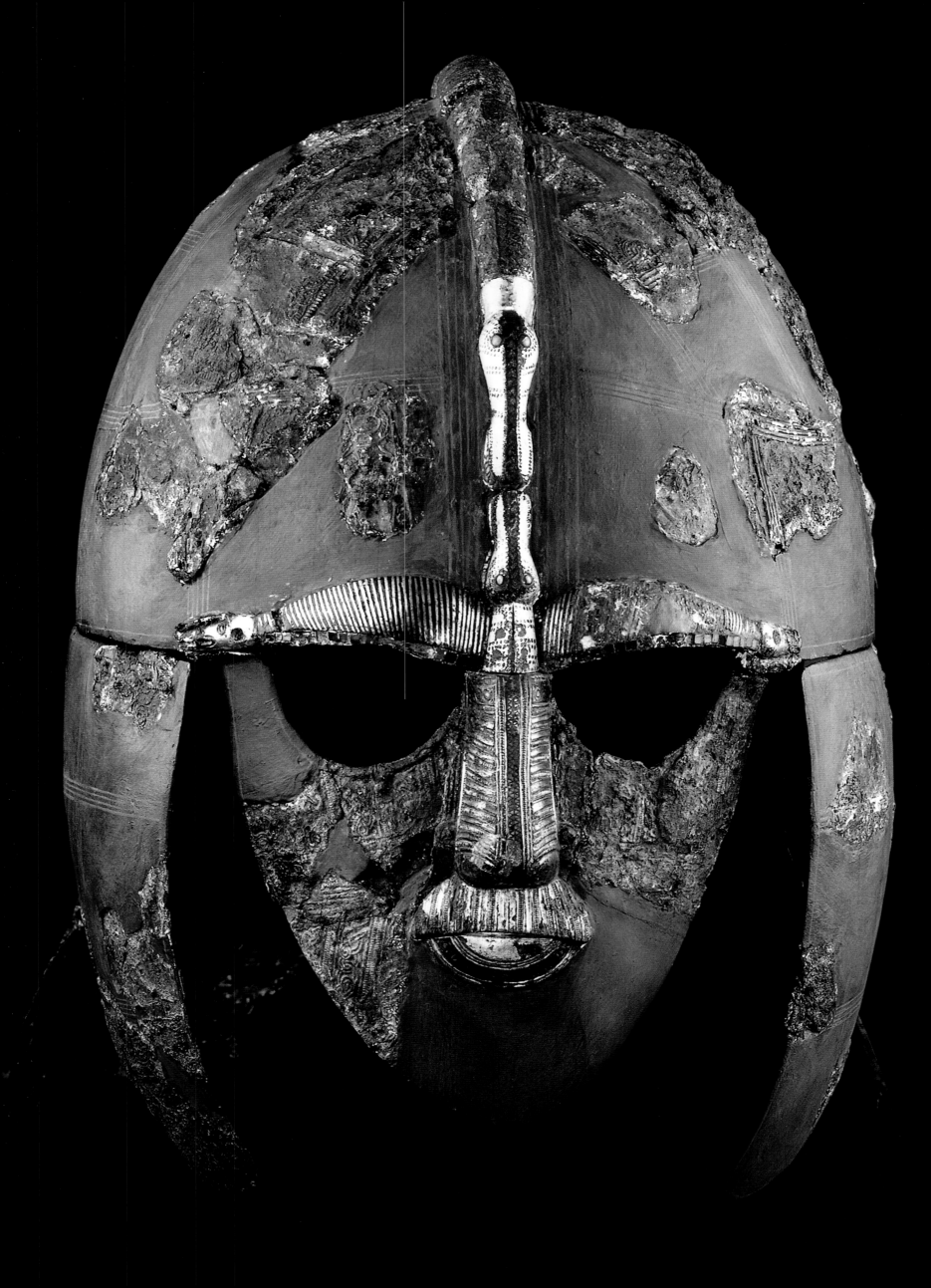

248 The Sutton Hoo ship burial, was excavated and photographed during the 1930s.

250 and 251 This helmet was shattered in 500 pieces when it was found at Sutton Hoo. Once restored, it was possible to reconstruct the complex decorations, including panels with zoomorphic designs and battle scenes in relief. An early reconstruction (below) placed the cheekpiece too low (British Museum, London).

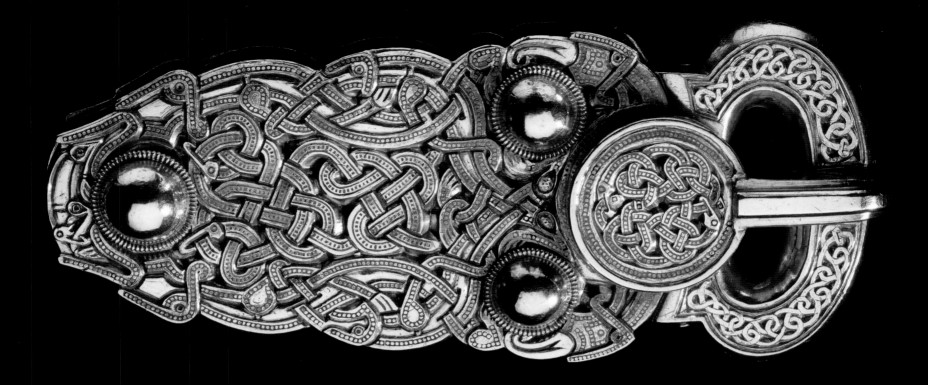

252 top This splendid gold buckle was among the grave goods of a high-ranking individual interred at the Sutton Hoo ship burial. The surface is completely covered with an intricate design of snakes coiled together (British Museum, London).

252-253 and 253 top These shoulder clasps found in the Sutton Hoo ship burial would have been used to hold together a leather cuirass worn by the deceased. They feature refined cloisonné ornamentation with panels covered in geometric designs and a border of ribbon animals, while the curved part depicts two interlocking boars (British Museum, London).

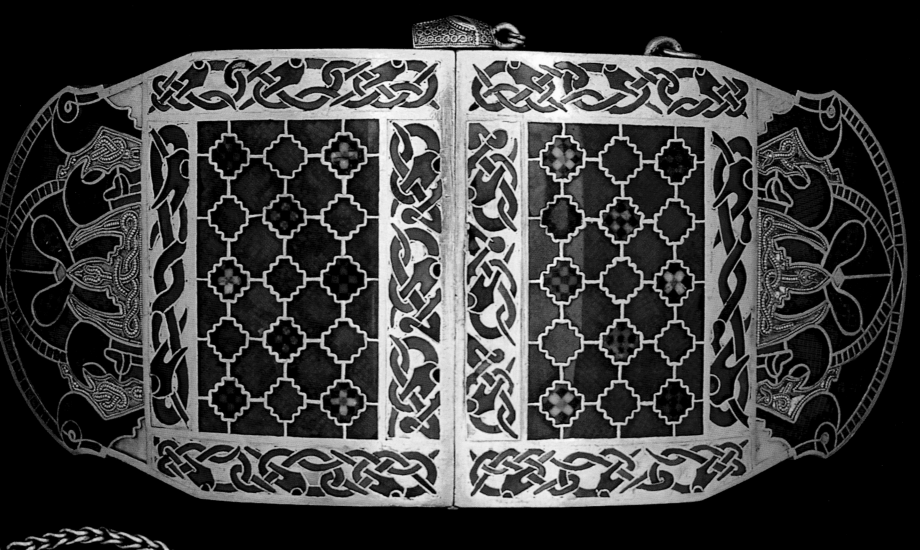

The Staffordshire Hoard:
The Gold of the Anglo-Saxons

On July 5, 2009, amateur archaeologist Terry Herbert made the find of a lifetime. Hunting with his metal detector on farmland in Staffordshire, England, he discovered the largest known hoard of Anglo-Saxon treasure, with nearly 1,700 objects, amounting to more than 11 lb (5 kg) of gold, many beautifully inlaid with garnets.

It is not just the size of the Staffordshire hoard that makes it important, but the type of objects included, and just as important, those it does not include. Almost all of the identifiable items are from male war gear: 86 pommel caps from swords or seaxes (short single-edged swords or knives), 135 sword hilt plates, and fragments from at least one helmet. There are also four, possibly five crosses of gold. One of the most significant pieces is a strip of gold with a Biblical inscription in Latin, taken from Numbers 10:35 or Psalm 68:1, which reads: "Rise up, o Lord, and may thy enemies be dispersed and those who hate thee be driven from thy face."

The elaborate and expensive decoration of the objects shows that they were created for the highest levels of Anglo-Saxon society, but there are no baldric fittings or large triangular buckles, representing male garb, and no dress fittings, brooches, or pendants representing female garb. Unlike the Anglo-Saxon royal burials at Sutton Hoo and Prittlewell, there are no furnishings, items of everyday use, or coins.

Archaeologists are seeking an explanation for the extraordinary composition of the Staffordshire hoard—almost exclusively male war gear—in its historical context. It appears to date to the 7th century, when a number of kingdoms were vying with each other in a state of semi-perpetual warfare, with the spread of

254-255 This gold band inscribed with a Biblical passage is among the most important items found in the Staffordshire Hoard. The style of lettering suggests that the object dates to the 8th or 9th century A.D. (Museum and Art Gallery, Birmingham).

255 top and bottom Many of the items in the Staffordshire Hoard are made of gold, with garnet cloisonné. This pommel cap (above) and this hilt collar (below) have some of the best decoration among the military items of this nature on display (Museum and Art Gallery, Birmingham).

Christianity occurring at the same time. An exact date is impossible to determine, but the inscription, the style of animal decoration, and similarities to the Sutton Hoo finds point to A.D. 650–700. as the best estimate. The hoard's findspot was near the heart of the Anglo-Saxon kingdom of Mercia, which at this time was expanding aggressively under a series of kings—Penda, Wulfhere, and Aethelred—fighting wars with the neighboring kingdoms of Northumbria and East Anglia.

The crosses in the hoard might offer a clue. The largest may have been an altar or processional cross, and had to be folded to be placed in hoard. Was the hoard perhaps buried by pagans? Penda was the last pagan king of Mercia, and he is known to have defeated and killed the Christian king Edwin of East Anglia in battle in A.D. 633. But at this period, Christians could equally despoil each other's shrines, so the connection is not a provable one.

Most of the gold and silver items were deliberately stripped from the objects to which they were originally attached, especially swords. But if it was being taken simply for the value of the gold, there would also be rich fittings from sword belts as at Sutton Hoo. Perhaps Staffordshire is a trophy hoard, the blades of the swords being remounted and reused. If so, it is impossible, however, to say if the hoard was the spoils from a single battle or one individual's long and successful military career.

Ultimately, we cannot say who the original owners were, who took it from them, and why or when they buried it. The Staffordshire Hoard remains a mystery in this regard.

But just as the discovery of Sutton Hoo in the 1930s required archaeologists of the time to reconsider their view of the era as a major decline from late Roman Britain, the Staffordshire hoard is showing today that we have underestimated the wealth and artistic genius of Anglo-Saxon society in the 7th century. (MR)

The Lost Goat:
The Dead Sea Scrolls Find

One of the greatest discoveries of the 20th century—the Dead Sea Scrolls, the oldest-known copies of the Hebrew Bible—was made without an archaeologist's trowel. In 1947, a wandering goat led a young Bedouin named Muhammad ed-Dib to clamber up the face of a cliff in the Judean Desert near the Dead Sea. Mid-pursuit, his attention was drawn to an unusual opening in its craggy limestone surface. As the story goes, ed-Dib was curious as to what may lie beyond the darkness of the cave, so he tossed a few small rocks inside. Instead of landing with a thud, as they would on the ground, the rocks landed with a sharp clink. Intrigued, he strained to discern the outlines of several cylindrical ceramic jars. The objects, however, frightened him. Fearing that desert *jinn*, or spirits, may inhabit the caves, he took off—too afraid, even, to gather his flock.

The next day he returned with companions from his Ta'amireh tribe who hoped the jars might be filled with gold and other treasures. Instead, while some jars were empty, others contained a jumble of rags enveloping brown leather wrappings that in turn swaddled manuscripts emblazoned on parchment in Hebrew, Aramaic, and Greek, none of which they could read. Though disappointed with the finds, the Bedouin kept the seven bundles they had recovered. They traveled with the scrolls for weeks, until they reached Jerusalem where they hoped to sell them to a local antiquities dealer by the name of Khalil Iskander Shahin, or "Kando." Equally unimpressed with the discoveries, Kando is reported to have left them on the floor of his adjacent cobbler's shop, hoping at least to use the leather to mend some shoes. But one day, on closer inspection, he became curious about the writing on the pages and brought them to St. Mark's monastery, part of Jerusalem's Syrian church. After the secretive visit, he started to believe that the scrolls might be of greater significance than he previously thought. So Kando recruited a friend, George Isaiah, and returned to the area of the cave to illicitly gather more. Eventually, they told the Syrian authorities, which led an archaeological expedition to the caves.

In the meantime, Kando came in contact with a Jewish scholar at Hebrew University, Professor Eleazar Sukenik, who is credited as being the first to see the potential value of the scrolls. In November 1947, Sukenik purchased three of them. He wanted to buy more, but Kando had already sold the other four to Mar Athanasius Yeshua Samuel, the Syrian Metropolitan of St. Marks, for £24 ($36). Samuel wisely brought his purchases to John Trever at the American School of Oriental Research in Jordanian Jerusalem, who photographed them. Along with William Brownlee and Millar Burrows, the school's director, Trever recognized the scrolls' date and contents. Archaeologist and epigrapher W.F. Albright, whom Trever consulted, confirmed them to be from time of King Herod. The discovery was announced worldwide on April 12, 1948.

In the years that followed, 10 additional caves were identified and investigated, and other scrolls were unearthed. As more and more people began to see, read, and hear about the texts, interest in them—and debates over them—intensified. To date, some 900 individual scrolls, all of which date from 3rd century B.C. to 1st century A.D., have come to light. Only years later, between 1988 and 1991, were the scrolls made available to the public.

Dating to the time when Jesus of Nazareth lived, the Dead Sea Scrolls are almost 1,000 years older than any other known Biblical texts. Some scholars believe the scrolls were written by male members of a Jewish religious sect known as the Essenes who lived at Qumran, a nearby settlement that thrived for 70 years until A.D. 31, when an earthquake struck, and again until A.D. 68, a turbulent time during the reign of King Herod. Others argue they were written elsewhere and hidden in the caves during a serious crisis. (EBM)

256 A naughty goat wandering up this craggy Judean Desert cliff face led the curious Bedouin who followed it to discover the Dead Sea Scrolls in a dark cave.

258 top The Dead Sea Scrolls were wrapped in leather and tucked into cylindrical ceramic jars such as this example. Ten were discovered in the first cave alone (Israel Museum, Jerusalem).

258 bottom The Temple Scroll was obtained by Israeli archaeologist and general Yigael Yadin during the 1967 Six-Day War from the Jerusalem antiquities dealer Kando, who had kept them in a shoebox for a decade (Israel Museum, Jerusalem).

259 At Jerusalem's Hebrew University in 1956, a German professor, James Biberkraut, unrolled the last of the original seven scrolls found in Cave 1, containing the Genesis Apocryphon.

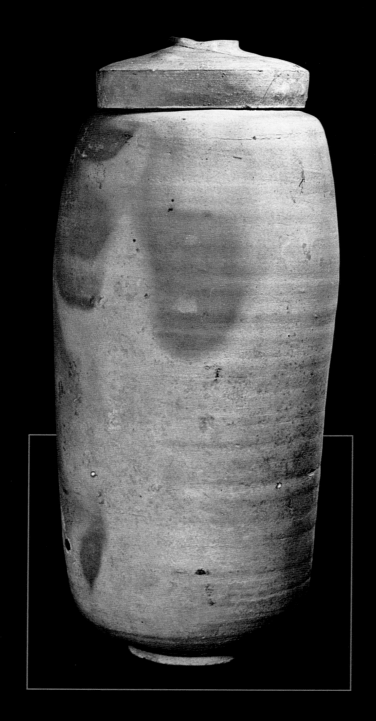

The Terracotta Army of the First Chinese Emperor

Dubbed "the eighth wonder of the ancient world," the 2,200-year-old terracotta army of Qin Shihuangdi, the first emperor of China, was brought to light in Shaanxi Province in March 1974, marking one of the few truly bright moments of the Cultural Revolution. This incredible chance discovery was made by farmers digging wells in search of water; instead, they were surprised to come across large pottery sherds.

The news quickly spread, and by July, archaeologists had begun formal excavations to investigate the site. Over the next few years, thousands of life-size—and eerily lifelike—terracotta warriors, along with their horses, chariots, and accoutrements, were uncovered from three enormous pits together spanning an area of 6 acres (22,000 sq m). (The entire burial complex, including the earthen mound covering what is believed to be the emperor's mausoleum, covers an area of 14 acres/56,000 sq m.) The remarkable finds revealed tangible remains of the stunning wealth and power of an emperor whose name and reputation alone were great enough to survive the millennia. Despite its humble beginnings, the discovery of the terracotta army at the ancient capital city of Xi'an is indeed one of the most extraordinary of the 20th century, and the world still waits with baited breath to see what will emerge from the ground next.

In 247 B.C., upon his father's death, Ying Zheng ascended the throne of the Zhou state of Qin at the age of nine. At first, he ruled with his mother and the help of important ministers. In his early 20s, however, he truly came into power, and began to conquer the six other existing states of ancient China—Qi, Chu, Yan, Han, Zhao, and Wei—through bloody, ruthless battles. In subsequent years, he went on to amass vast territories as far east as the Yangzi River and as far south as Vietnam. In 221 B.C., after his final great victory, he ultimately declared himself the "first emperor" of the unified state of Qin; literally, "Qin Shihuangdi."

For years he maintained sway over an impressive territory that included 36 prefectures that were further divided into counties and townships, and administered by civil and military officials through a central bureaucracy. In some respects, he was a great ruler who can be credited for centralizing the state, abolishing the feudal system, and building critical infrastructure, including roads and canals. He even converted mounds of rammed earth along the empire's northern frontier into a defensive system to deflect invading nomads, thus creating the first real iteration of the Great Wall. But he was also known for his ruthlessness and cruelty.

The construction of his funerary complex is believed to have taken some three and a half decades and nearly three quarters of a million men to complete. When it was finished, those involved in its design and construction were allegedly buried alive inside.

The emperor's actual tomb—believed to be located under a nearly 164-ft (50-m) high earthen mound about 1 mile (1.5 km) from the terracotta army—has not yet been excavated. Hower, according to legend, as well as written records, including those by the 1st-century B.C. historian Sima Qian, on Qin Shihuangdi's death in 210 B.C., the emperor was laid to rest in a tomb that re-created the entire universe. The lavish underground interpretation of heaven and earth, complete with models of palaces and buildings, was eternally illuminated with whale-oil-filled lamps. The light must have glistened in the pearls that dotted the ceiling, representing the constellations, which were surrounded by jade ornaments and green feathers. Throughout his final resting place flowed mechanically powered mercury symbolizing the great Yangzi and Yellow rivers, as well as the ocean. (Soil samples taken by researchers have confirmed the presence of the element.) The tomb itself was surrounded by walls, towers, temples, and administrative buildings, the descriptions say, and it was reportedly rigged with automatic crossbows to stop grave robbers dead in their tracks.

Guarding this impressive funerary complex was the now-famous terracotta army of unblinking men and horses, symbolically accom-

260 Though only about one-third of it has been excavated, Pit 1 at Xi'an is believed to contain an estimated 6,000 terracotta warriors and horses, as well as 40 battle chariots.

262 Only a few years after the death of Qin Shihuangdi, a rebel named Xiang Yu set fire to the emperor's palace and funerary complex, causing the roof to collapse and damage to the terracotta army.

262-263 Chinese archaeologists work in Pit 1 in the 1970s. Most of the figures excavated from this location were infantrymen. Measuring 755 ft (230 m) from east to west and 204 ft (62 m) from north to south, Pit 1 covers a total area of more than 3.5 acres (14,000 sq m).

panying their fearless leader to a glorious afterlife, which he believed to be filled with the riches and prestige he enjoyed in his lifetime. Archaeologists have partially excavated three pits—each some 17–23 ft (5–7 m) below the ground—brimming with the haunting clay warriors. The layout of each pit is basically the same: standing on roads paved with bricks made of pottery, the figures were stationed in corridors separated by rammed-earth walls, covered by a roof of wooden rafters over which fiber mats, tiles, and soil were placed. But their contents varied in intriguing ways.

In 1974, archaeologists unearthed a portion of Pit 1, the largest of the three, which was discovered by the well-diggers. Covering an area of approximately 4 acres (14,000 sq m), the rectangular pit contained the army's main force of infantrymen, many of whom clutched actual bronze weapons. While only a third of the pit has been excavated, it is estimated to have been stocked with some 6,000 warriors and horses. Two years later, archaeologists began investigating the L-shaped Pit 2, which housed specialized military troops in complex battle formation, including standing archers; war chariots originally made of wood (now deteriorated) and charioteers; cavalrymen, each of whom stands in front of a saddled horse holding its reins in his right hand and a bow in his left; and archers. Also in 1976, archaeolo-

gists unearthed the U-shaped Pit 3. Although it is the smallest of the three pits, measuring only 560 sq ft (520 sq m), it is believed to represent the "command headquarters," holding 68 pottery guards of honor and a chariot drawn by 4 horses. In total, researchers estimate, the pits were stocked with some 8,000 terracotta warriors and horses. To date, not a single one has been found intact.

The entire phantom army was divided into low-, middle-, and high-ranking soldiers. Located to the east of the emperor's mausoleum, the warriors stood guard facing east in perpetuity, with their backs to the tomb, ready to strike at the first sign of invaders…or, perhaps, grave robbers.

The terracotta figures were made with local clay—carefully sifted, washed, and combined with ground quartz for a uniform appearance —from prefabricated, interchangeable body parts. While the heads, arms, and torsos of both the men and horses were hollow, their legs were solid so the figures would be well balanced. When it came to the faces, however, each was individually carved with a sharp bamboo reed, so that no two were the same. The craftsmen's names were inscribed on back of the figures' robes, legs, or armor; some 80 different ones are known today. While the figures now appear to have a very similar appearance, they were originally painted in a wide array of colors, including blue, green, pink, vermilion, and white.

Since the late 1990s, excavations in newly discovered pits have revealed additional spectacular treasures, including 120 suits of stone armor and nine stone helmets; a set of playful and expressive figures who likely served as acrobats in the emperor's court; a group of men representing mid-level civil officers with knives and sharpeners tied to their waists, which would have been used as erasers on wood or bamboo; and an F-shaped pit full of bronze cranes and geese affixed to pedestals. Recently, the excavation of Pit 1 has also been resumed.

Later in his life, Qin Shihuangdi became obsessed with a quest for immortality, whose secrets he believed lay in the legendary mountains of Peng Lai, Fong Zhang, and Ying Zhou where the immortals lived. Although he never found that promising spot, when he died at the age of 50, his legacy certainly took on a new life. (EBM)

264-265 The warriors are all about 6 ft (1.8 m) tall and were originally painted in an array of bright colors. In Pit 1, they were placed on floors made of clay bricks, lined up in battle formation between walls of rammed earth. Throught the complex ran an elaborate underground system of pipes and cisterns.

266 The terracotta army was made of local clay and fired between 1,742 and 1,922°F (950 and 1,050°C). They vary in weight from 240 to 660 lb (110 to 300 kg).

267 The rank of each soldier is reflected his dress. Cavalrymen such as this one wore tight-fitting clothing, including helmets with straps under their chins, which would have been ideal riding attire, over which a flowing robe could have been donned.

268-269 Many of the terracotta warriors held real bronze weapons, including double-edged swords coated with .6 to 2 percent chromium, which protected them against corrosion.

270 In a pit to the west of the emperor's mausoleum, archaeologists discovered two teams of bronze war chariots and horses, each produced at approximately half-life-size. Unearthed between 1978 and 1980, they were originally buried in a large wooden coffin, which has since decomposed.

271 The "Comfortable Chariot" contained diamond-shaped holes in the carriage for ventilation, which ensured a cool ride. Though the pit had not been looted, the chariots were found in thousands of pieces, which took eight years to reconstruct (Qinshihuang Terracotta Figures Museum).

272-273 The bodies of the terracotta warriors were mass-produced, but their facial features were individually carved by hand with a sharp stick of bamboo. No two figures, including this soldier and officer, are alike (Qinshihuang Terracotta Figures Museum).

Underwater Greek Masterpieces:
The Riace Bronzes

When amateur scuba diver Stefano Mariottini glimpsed a human hand poking out of the seafloor off the coast of Riace in southeastern Italy, he initially feared he had made a grisly discovery. But the chemist, a vacationer from Rome, enjoying some downtime in the summer of 1972 in nearby Reggio Calabria, soon realized that the body part actually belonged to a bronze statue—one of two promptly brought to the surface by Italian archaeological authorities.

These incomparable works stand out as among the most magnificent masterpieces of classical Greek art to be recovered in Italy in the 20th century. They are recognized not only for their exquisite details and expert craftsmanship, but also for their rarity, as most bronzes were melted down in antiquity so the valuable material could be reused. The two larger-than-life-size statues, later unceremoniously dubbed "A" and "B" by researchers, thus add a wealth of information to our knowledge of classical bronze sculpture, which previously was known primarily from Roman copies in marble.

Standing at about 7 ft (2 m) apiece, the towering nude male statues with rippling pectoral muscles and slender, almost effeminate legs are believed to represent either warriors or gods. They are also widely thought to be part of a larger group, perhaps commemorating a military victory, once displayed at Olympia or Delphi in Greece. Their sparkling eyes are inlaid with glass and bone (or perhaps ivory); their lashes and teeth are fashioned of silver; and their nipples and lips are kissed with copper. Both bearded figures once held weapons and shields (now missing), but only statue "B," thought to depict a man older than statue "A," dons a helmet. Some suggest "A" may have worn a wreath atop his mop of thick, curly hair.

The Riace Bronzes are so exquisite that scholars have argued they were crafted by, among others, Pheidias, the renowned Greek sculptor and architect who is responsible for decorating the Parthenon on the Acropolis in Athens. Cast between 460 and 430 B.C., the works were likely deposited in their 30-ft (9-m) deep resting place as they were being transported by ship from Greece during a raging storm. However, since the remains of a wreck were never recovered, scholars have noted the possibility that the statues may have been purposefully dumped to lessen the weight of a founding vessel.

An even larger mystery, however, surrounds this particular discovery. In recent years, local "art sleuth" Giuseppe Braghò has claimed that the statues were unearthed with their spears and shields intact, and that there may even have been a third figure. Pointing to photographic and audio evidence from the day the statues were brought to the surface—including a statement Mariottini made the day after the discovery in which he refers to "a group of statues"—he insists that the other items were stolen and could perhaps have wound up in the collection of the Getty Museum in Los Angeles, an accusation that the prominent U.S. institution flatly denies.

A March 2007 statement on the Getty's website reads as follows: "In recent weeks, there have been reports in the press suggesting that pieces from the Bronzes of Riace (a shield, lance, and helmet) might currently reside at the J. Paul Getty Museum. This information is wrong and should be corrected. These objects, that are suggested to be part of the Riace Bronzes, have never been in the Getty Museum's collection." The following year, Italy's Culture Minister Francesco Rutelli undertook a new investigation of the site, following reports that a U.S. ship had spotted pieces of metal underwater near the statues' findspot.

After the completion of their conservation in 1981, the famed Riace Bronzes were displayed in Rome, Florence, and Milan. But that is the last time they left Calabria—except on an envelope. The figures were showcased on a commemorative stamp that year, but they have remained in the collection of the National Museum of Reggio Calabria, where they draw some 130,000 visitors annually. (EBM)

274 Simply dubbed "A" and "B" by present-day researchers, the exquisite Riace Bronzes provide a rare glimpse at the extraordinary craftsmanship of classical Greek bronzes, which were often melted down in antiquity so the precious metal could be reused (National Museum, Reggio Calabria).

276 Statue "B," believed to represent the older of the two figures, once wore a helmet, which was tipped back in the style of an Athenian warrior (National Museum, Reggio Calabria).

277 The excitement mounted as crowds gathered in 1972 to witness the larger-than-life Riace Bronzes surface after 2,500 years on the seafloor.

New Frontiers in Archaeology

Since the invention of radiocarbon dating in 1949, the advancement of science and development of new technologies have revolutionized archaeological research and investigations. In the past, the thrill of discovery could only be achieved through weeks and months in the field, but today's archaeologists can learn about a site thousands of miles away. And archaeology is conducted on scales ranging from molecules to entire landscapes.

Throughout our lives, the food we eat and substances to which we are exposed leave their signatures on our tissues, including our bones and teeth. Today we travel frequently over long distances and consume foods grown around the world, but this was not so in the past. This simple fact gives archaeologists a powerful tool. For example, Sir Flinders Petrie discovered a 17th Dynasty (1641–1539 B.C.) royal mummy at Qurna, Egypt, in 1909. Encased in an elaborate coffin, the mummy of a young woman wore a magnificent gold collar, gold earrings and bracelets, and a girdle of fine electrum rings as well as a scarab. Other items buried with her included six Nubian pots. The elaborate burial, partially legible inscriptions on the coffin, and location of the burial all indicate she was a queen. The pottery was taken by some as evidence she was Nubian and had been married to a pharaoh in a dynastic match. But the analysis of strontium isotopes in her remains proves she grew up in Egypt, not Nubia.

With the 5,300-year-old "Iceman", also known as Ötzi, found in the Alps in 1991, researchers have reached even more conclu-

sions. The chemistry (oxygen isotopes) of the Iceman's teeth and bones shows he spent more of his time in lower valleys when he was young, but at higher altitudes later in life. The strontium-to-lead ratios in his teeth were found to match most closely the Eisack Valley, northeast of present-day Bolzano, Italy, suggesting that's where he lived as a child. But the most incredible revelation, from a science perspective, came from studying small flecks of mica found in his gut. These, presumably from the stone used to grind his bread flour, could be dated to about 100 million years ago. That matches the date of such stone from the Vinschgau Mountains some 30 miles (50 km) from his presumed birthplace.

For decades we have been able to glean more information about the ancient world than ever could have been imagined by the pioneers of archaeology. Howard Carter may have excavated Tutankhamun in 1922, but it was only in 2009 that the young pharaoh's DNA, his genetic fingerprint, was successfully extracted and analyzed. Although the interpretation of those results—and of members of Tut's extended family—may be debated, DNA studies have opened a whole new chapter of archaeology. Interestingly, genetic evidence of malaria was found in Tutankhamun. Elsewhere, researchers are sampling tuberculosis (TB) DNA from ancient and historical human remains and comparing it with the modern TB-causing bacteria in an effort to understand the evolution of this killer. DNA studies are also charting our own evolution, providing evi-

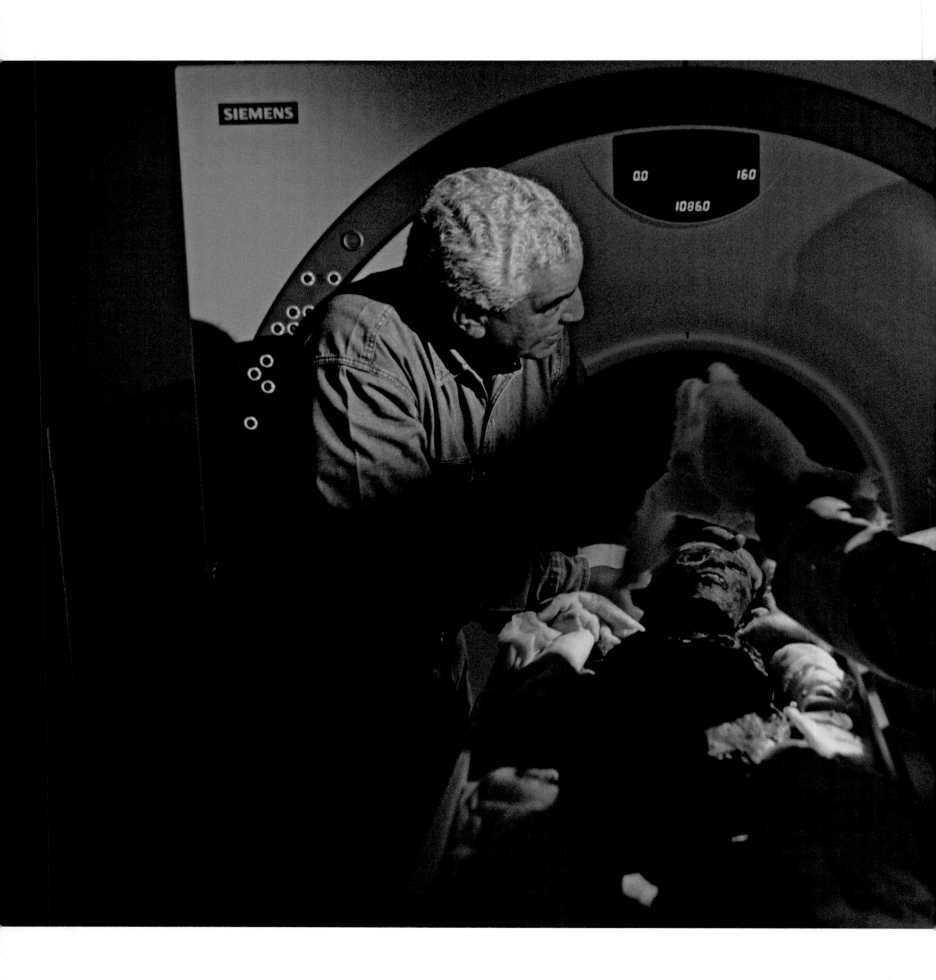

280-281 In 2005, the mummy of Tutankhamun underwent a CT scan at a laboratory outside his tomb in the Valley of the Kings. Zahi Hawass assists the technicians shortly before the testing begins.

dence of our migration out of Africa and, now, for the mixing of Neanderthal and modern human genetic pools.

There is also the richness and depth of knowledge about a site and its artifacts that can be achieved today, which many of the early great archaeologists could never have predicted. In 1920, James Henry Breasted, the first American to obtain his Ph.D. in Egyptology, purchased an 8th-century B.C. mummy in Egypt for the Oriental Institute's fledgling museum. Mummy unwrapping demonstrations were popular spectacles in Breasted's day, but the one he brought back was spared that fate because of her exquisitely painted *cartonnage* (linen and plaster coffin). In 2009, the mummy, named Meresamun, was examined using a 256-slice CT scanner, becoming the first mummy ever subject to such advanced technology. Researchers were able to virtually peel back the layers of her coffin, mummy wrappings, skin, and bones, to reveal information about how she looked—with an overbite and prominent cheekbones—and that the priestess-musician led an active lifestyle. Over the course of the hour-long scan, some 30 billion individual measurements were obtained, which have been used to create remarkable 3-D digital images of every inch of her body.

Imaging can also be done on a larger scale, documenting and preserving archaeological sites and monuments digitally using Light Detection and Ranging (LiDAR), which creates 3-D maps that can be rotated and viewed from any angle. For large monuments, such as Maya temples, LiDAR can record tens of millions of data points, the coordinates of which can be related to one another to within a millimeter. For buildings or other structures facing environmental degradation or even destruction, for example, by an earthquake, LiDAR offers the possibility of making a record that is a far more accurate than anything that could be produced by hand measurements, and much faster than traditional surveying methods. This type of scanning is now being used worldwide, from the hulks of Gold Rush-era steamboats on the Yukon River, to Easter Island's giant statues, to the massive Olmec stone heads, to 12th-century A.D. mud-brick structures at the ancient city of Merv in Turkmenistan.

While a valuable tool for researching sites and monuments, LiDAR also could provide a last-chance record for heritage sites threatened by conflict. It could have been used to digitally preserve Afghanistan's famous Bamiyan Buddhas, Which were destroyed by the Taliban.

Today, archaeologists can use a number of means to see beneath the soil without ever digging. These methods are usually termed "geophysical prospecting" as opposed to "remote sensing," which includes aerial and satellite imagery. The results from geophysical prospecting can be transformational, for example at Etowah, a major Native American site in Georgia; subsurface mapping tools have mandated a complete revision of archaeologists' understanding of the site. Etowah was a premier site of the Mississippian societies that dominated much of the continent from eastern Oklahoma to northern Florida from about A.D. 1000 to 1500. The largest earthen mound at the site stands higher than a six-story building. Using a suite of equipment to measure underground magnetism, density, and electrical properties, researchers employed portable sensors—some handheld, some dragged over the ground on wheeled "sleds"—to map subtle variations, or anomalies, in the soil. They have identified a total of 140 buildings, from dense clusters of houses around small plazas to some very large buildings, including one structure that's over 100 ft (30 m) on one side. They also found that Mound A, the largest at the site, had at least four sizeable structures atop it and a courtyard that dated to the height of Etowah's power between A.D. 1325 and 1375. Geophysical prospecting can eliminate the need for extensive test trenches and minimize the amount of actual digging, speeding the accurate interpretation of sites and reducing costs of archaeological expeditions.

At the University of Chicago's Oriental Institute, a team under the acronym CAMEL (Center for Ancient Middle Eastern Landscapes) has been working since 1998 to digitally combine archives of topographic maps dating from the mid-19th century to the present, aerial photos from the 1920s and the 1950s, and remote-sensing data such as declassified U.S. spy satellite images to create a picture of the land-

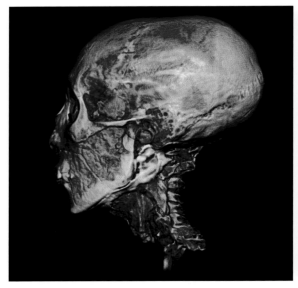
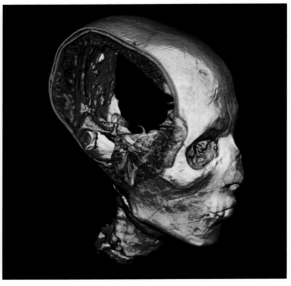

282 top and 283 The face of Tutankhamun, who died in 1323 B.C., was re-created by Elisabeth Daynes, a facial reconstruction expert considered one of the best paleoartists in the world, based on scans of the young pharaoh's body.

282 bottom The computerized images from the CT scan of Tutankhamun's mummy revealed elements that had not been readily available through simple visual analysis, such as a cleft palate.

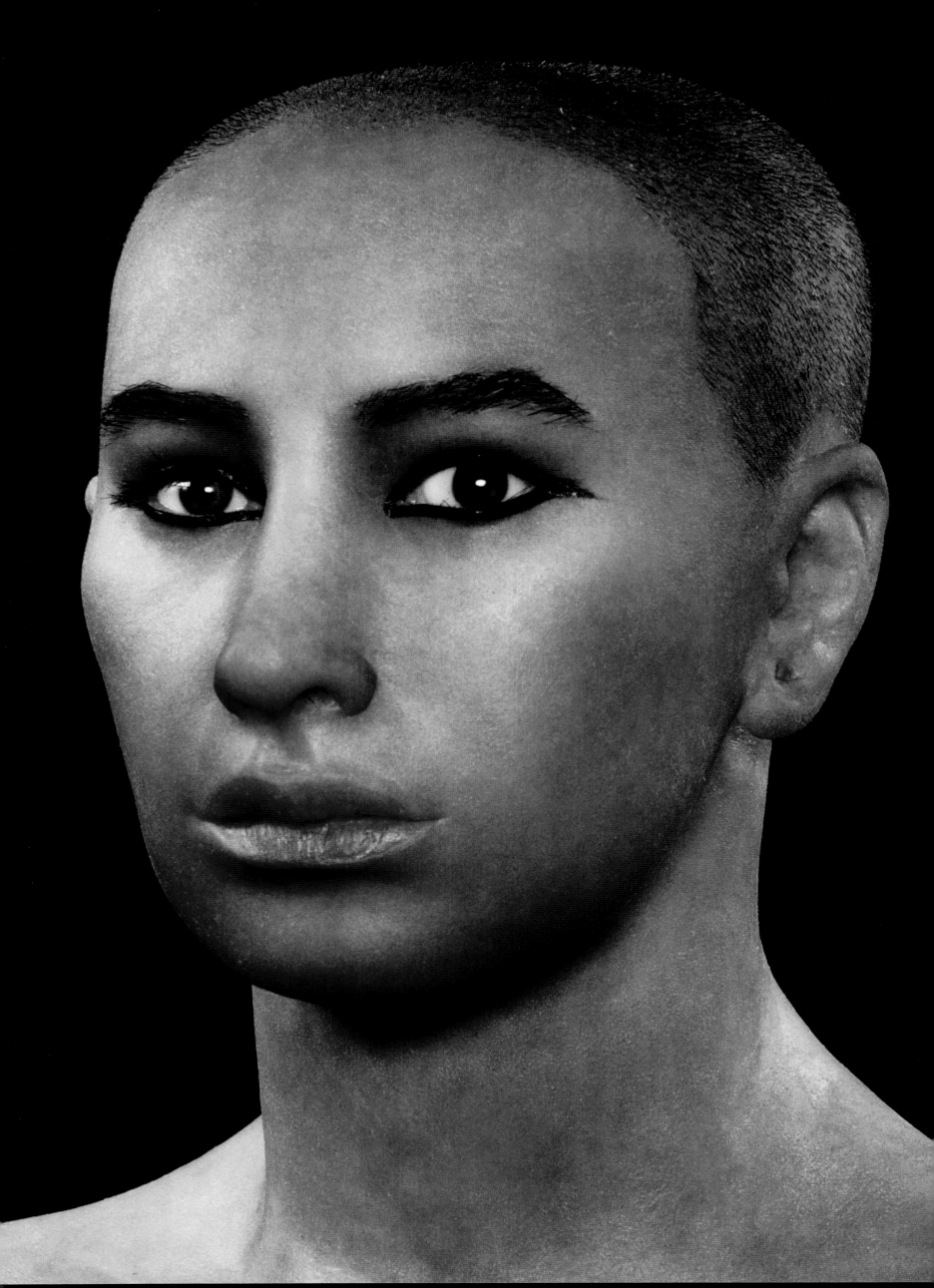

scape of the Middle East. From their personal computers, archaeologists working (or planning to work) in the region—from Greece to Afghanistan to the Horn of Africa—can clearly visualize how the area surrounding a site has changed over the past centuries. This information is critical in a region whose landscape has changed dramatically since the mid-20th century as mechanized farming techniques, urban development, and modern warfare have obscured sites and features that had survived for millennia. Each composite image has endless applications, including the ability to overlay real-time GPS data on it, so archaeologists in the field using a tablet PC can actually see themselves on an image of the site or landscape.

Finally, there is deep-water archaeology. One of the greatest maritime disasters was the sinking of RMS *Titanic* on April 14, 1912, after the ship struck an iceberg in the North Atlantic. Of the 2,223 passengers and crew, 1,517 drowned. A French and American expedition located the remains of *Titanic* in 1985 with side-scan sonar and the wreck was filmed using an unmanned submersible. The following year, explorer Bob Ballard returned to *Titanic* in a submersible, the only way to reach the remains on the seafloor at a depth of about 12,500 ft (3,800 m).

Ballard refused to bring any artifacts up from *Titanic*, considering the wreck to be a gravesite. Commercial firms, including RMS Titanic Inc., did recover, controversially, some 6,000 artifacts. Ballard and others have documented damage to the wreck caused by careless operation of submersibles or ROVs (remotely operated vehicles) as well as the removal of key items such as the bell from its mast.

Titanic highlights the development of technology that makes the deepest wrecks accessible and the inherent conflict in applying maritime salvage laws to historic and archaeological remains. Ethical archaeologists and commercial salvors who strip wrecks of artifacts and then sell them with little or no study, publication, or appropriate conservation or curatorial efforts have no common ground. A new UNESCO (United Nations Educational, Scientific and Cultural Organization) convention may provide the necessary international framework for protecting such submerged cultural heritage. (MR)

284-285 Modern technology, such as digital image acquisition through scanners, is an important part of the work done by archaeologists. Here, a team directed by William Saturno performs a scan of the oldest Maya mural known today. It was found in 2001 at San Bartolo, Guatemala, and has been dubbed the "Maya Sistine Chapel."

Index

Photo credits